MAA • 515

Armies of the First Carlist War 1833–39

Gabriele Esposito • Illustrated by Giuseppe Rava

Series editor Martin Windrow

Osprey Publishing c/o Bloomsbury Publishing Plc
PO Box 883, Oxford, OX1 9PL, UK
Or:
c/o Bloomsbury Publishing Inc
1385 Broadway, 5th Floor, New York, NY 10018, USA
E-mail: info@ospreypublishing.com

www.ospreypublishing.com

OSPREY is a trademark of Osprey Publishing Ltd, a division of Bloomsbury
Publishing Plc.

First published in Great Britain in 2017

A CIP catalogue record for this book is available from the British Library

ISBN: PB: 978 1 47282 523 0
ePub: 978 1 47282 524 7
ePDF: 978 1 47282 525 4
XML: 978 1 47282 526 1

17 18 19 20 21   10 9 8 7 6 5 4 3 2 1

Editor: Martin Windrow
Index by Alan Rutter
Typeset in Helvetica Neue and ITC New Baskerville
Page layouts by PDQ Digital Media Solutions, Bungay, UK
Printed in China through World Print Ltd

Osprey Publishing supports the Woodland Trust, the UK's leading woodland
conservation charity. Between 2014 and 2018 our donations are being spent on
their Centenary Woods project in the UK.

To find out more about our authors and books, visit www.ospreypublishing.com.
Here you will find extracts, author interviews, details of forthcoming events, and
the option to sign up for our newsletter.

Dedication

To my parents Maria Rosaria and Benedetto, for their love, advice and practical
support throughout the preparation of this book.
This work is also dedicated to the memory of all the brave Spanish soldiers who
fought and died for their ideals during the First Carlist War.

Acknowledgements

Special thanks are due to the series editor Martin Windrow, for his support
during the research and writing of this book; to Giuseppe Rava, for the passion
and generosity which he has brought to the task of illustrating it; and to Ralph
Weaver and The Continental Wars Society, for helping me in researching some
essential materials. In particular I wish to express my admiration for Conrad
Cairns and his pioneering studies on this subject.

All the pictures published in this book are in the public domain, obtained from
the Digital Collections of the New York Public Library (Vinkhuijzen Collection of
Military Uniforms), or from Wikipedia Commons:

https://digitalcollections.nypl.org/collections/the-vinkhuijzen-collection-of-
military-uniforms#/?tab=navigation
http://commons.wikimedia.org/wiki
The map was obtained from: http://www.d-maps.com/index.php?lang=en

ARTIST'S NOTE

Readers may care to note that the original paintings from which the colour
plates in this book were prepared are available for private sale. All reproduction
copyright whatsoever is retained by the Publisher. All enquiries should be
addressed to:

Giuseppe Rava, via Borgotto 17, 48018 Faenze (RA), Italy
info@g-rava.it

The Publishers regret that they can enter into no correspondence upon
this matter.

OPPOSITE
Ramón Cabrera, commandant-general of the Carlist Army of the Centre; he is portrayed wearing the Carlist *boina* cap, and a pelisse jacket made of fleece of contrasting colours and weights. The son of a fisherman, Cabrera had studied to become a priest before the war, but would come to be called 'the Tiger of Maestrazgo'. He proved himself second only to Zumalacárregui among Carlist commanders, and in 1838 his army outclassed the declining Army of the North. Cabrera created and ruled a genuine Carlist 'mini-state' in Aragon, establishing his capital in the city of Morella. After this fell to Gen Espartero's regulars on 30 May 1840, on 6 July Cabrera followed 8,000 of his men across the border into French exile. He would return to Spain in 1848 to lead insurgents during the Second Carlist War; defeated once again, he died in England in 1877, after declining to participate in the Third War.

ARMIES OF THE FIRST CARLIST WAR 1833–39

INTRODUCTION

The history of 19th-century Spain was characterized by political turmoil punctuated by three bloody civil conflicts, known as the Carlist Wars. Essentially, these were fought between two main factions not only over the succession to the Spanish throne, but over two different visions of Spain's future. On one side were the 'Liberals', with (by the standards of the time) a progressive programme for a constitutional monarchy: they were opposed by the ultra-conservative 'Carlists', seeking the return of an absolute monarchy buttressed by the Catholic Church.

In 1812, during the exile of King Ferdinand VII and Napoleon's occupation of Spain (1808–14), the *juntas* which sprang up to oppose the French passed a liberal constitution. After his first restoration Ferdinand devoted almost his whole reign to trying to crush the progessive factions, and several revolts were suppressed by force of arms – in 1823, even by those of French troops sent to Ferdinand's aid by Louis XVIII. Thereafter French troops remained in Spain for several years, while all free political expression was suppressed.

Uncertainty over the succession dominated Ferdinand's last years; since he had no son, his brother Don Carlos had long expected to succeed. In 1829, however, Ferdinand decided to marry again in hope of fathering a direct heir, and the following year he announced the existence of a document signed by his father Carlos IV in 1789, which made any male *or female* child the legitimate heir. He also proclaimed an amnesty, which brought back to Spain many exiled liberals. In October 1830 Ferdinand's new queen, Maria Christina, bore him a daughter who was named Isabella. The supporters of Don Carlos refused to accept the child as the righful successor, but when Ferdinand died on 29 September 1833 his infant daughter was proclaimed Queen of

Spain under the regency of her mother. Refusing to accept this, on 1 October Don Carlos had himself proclaimed as the legitimate King Carlos V.

The years 1808–14 had implanted a strong tradition of guerrilla resistance in many parts of the country, and in the weeks that followed Don Carlos's proclamation his supporters in many provinces started to organize insurgent groups that launched attacks against the Queen Regent's forces. The conflict soon escalated into all-out civil war; the 'Carlists' began to create an army in the rural highlands of northern Spain, where they had complete control of the territory and unconditional support from the local population and clergy. The regular soldiers fighting against them soon became known as 'Cristinos' or 'Isabelinos', from the names of their regent and infant queens.

Facing opposition from all the conservative sections of Spanish society, Maria Christina had to seek the help of the more moderate among the liberals, who acquired increasing influence over the royal government. Reforms enacted by Maria Christina during 1834 placed some limits on the power of the monarchy, and the government party began to be known simply as 'Liberals'. (In fact, they were a coalition of different groups; more radical factions would confiscate Church property. A violent rupture in July–August 1836 saw troops mutiny and several generals executed, leading to a new, more progressive constitution.) The Queen Regent also enjoyed the active support of Britain, France and Portugal, in the Quadruple Alliance agreed on 22 April 1834.

CHRONOLOGY

1833:

October–November Carlist risings in Galicia, Vizcaya, Guipúzcoa, Alava, Navarre, Old Castile, La Rioja, Aragon, Catalonia and Extremadura; mostly crushed by Liberal forces, including at Los Arcos **(11 Oct)** and Peñacerrada **(19 Nov)**.

December Liberal Gen Espartero defeats guerrillas in Valencia **(25th)**; Gen Lorenzo defeats Basque commander Zumalacárregui at Astarta **(29th)**, but fails to prevent his escape.

1834:

March Zumalacárregui's attack on Vitoria fails. Liberal Gen Quesada carries out harsh reprisals in north.

April Guerrilla leader Cabrera achieves successes in Aragon, but another, Carnicer, is defeated at Mayals **(11th)**. Zumalacárregui defeats Gen Lorenzo at Abárzuza **(22nd)**.

May-July Liberals in north concentrate on defending cities and keeping roads open, and establish defensive line Pamplona–Vitoria. Zumalacárregui controls much of countryside, and raids freely.

July Don Carlos, who had been fighting in the Portuguese civil war, joins his supporters in the north.

August Zumalacárregui ambushes Gen de Carondelet at Peñas de San Fausto **(19th)**, and inflicts heavy losses even when driven off by Gen Rodil at Artaza **(31st)**.

4 September Small but significant cavalry victory by Carlists at Viana.

27-28 October Zumalacárregui uses conventional battle array to beat Brig O'Doyle at Salvatierra.

12 December In largest pitched battle yet, Zumalacárregui's 10,000 men are beaten by Gens Córdova's and Oráa's larger forces at Mendazà, but divided Liberal commands fail to coordinate pursuit.

1835:

2–3 January Though greatly outnumbered, Zumalacárregui's army shows capability in conventional tactics to win actions at Ormáiztegui and Segura.

2 February During campaign to ensure access to French border, Zumalacárregui holds pass at Arquinjas against Gen Lorenzo.

March–April Liberal Gen Espoz y Mina's Pamplona offensive fails. String of Carlist successes increase recruiting, fill arsenals and raise morale. Liberals seek foreign help.

May Zumalacárregui lays siege to Villafranca del Oria, and repels relief attempt by Gen Oráa at Larrainzar **(29th)**.

June Gen Córdova's relief attempt beaten off at Descarga **(2nd)**. Villafranca falls **(3rd)**, yielding large military stores. Vizcaya and Guipúzcoa entirely in Carlist hands except for capital cities. Zumalacárregui urges advance on Madrid via Vitoria, but Don Carlos insists on besieging Bilbao **(10th)**. Zumalacárregui mortally wounded **(15th)** and dies **(24th)**. Gen Gonzáles Moreno appointed to command Army of North; siege abandoned.

July First elements of British Auxiliary Legion arrive to aid Liberals.

16 July Decisive victory by Liberal Gen Córdova's 36,000 men over Moreno's 24,000 at Mendigorria, but not exploited.

Map showing the provinces of Spain. During 1834–40 most of the fighting took place in the north: the Basque provinces (Vizcaya, Guipúzcoa and Alava), Navarre, La Rioja, Old Castile, Aragon and Catalonia. However, one Carlist expedition – led by Gen Miguel Gómez in June–December 1836 – ranged across 2,800 miles, from Galicia all the way south to Algeciras at the tip of Andalusia, before returning to Bilbao in Vizcaya. The royalists tried to hold defensive lines anchored on cities and rivers, but field armies often found themselves playing hide-and-seek in open country. (Map modified by author; original from http://www.d-maps.com/carte.php?num_car=2211&lang=it)

August–December Liberals and Carlists both consolidate territories defensively.

August Arrival of French Foreign Legion to aid Liberals. Carlists launch first of series of speculative expeditions into Liberal-held provinces, led by Brig Guergué into Aragon and Catalonia.

11 November Don Carlos appoints Cabrera commandant-general in Aragon.

1836:

Spring Carlists make several unsuccessful attempts on Liberal strongholds on northern coast. Driven off by Gen Espartero at Orduña **(5 March)**, and by British Auxiliary Legion at Ayetta **(5 May)**.

June Gen Garcia leads Carlist expedition into Old Castile. Failed Carlist attacks on San Sebastián **(6th & 9th)**.

26 June–19 December Gen Miguel Gómez leads 4,000-man Carlist expedition across whole country, from Galicia to southern Andalusia; cooperates with Army of Centre to take towns; captures many weapons from National Militia; defeats Royal Guard sortie from Madrid; recruits 4 new battalions; and avoids other Liberal armies, returning safely to Basque provinces. Meanwhile:

July–August Violent Liberal political upheavals; Gen Espartero succeeds Córdova as commander in north.

October–December Second Carlist siege of Bilbao, relieved by Espartero on Christmas Day.

1837:

10–16 March Liberals' converging three-prong Oriamendi offensive fails due to Carlist mobility over interior lines.

15 May–26 October Greatest Carlist offensive – Don Carlos leads 'Royal Expedition' with 12,200 men into Catalonia, then crosses Ebro **(29 June)** to link with Cabrera's Army of Centre in Aragon. Carlist victories at Huesca **(24 May)** and Barbastro **(2 June)**; defeats at Grá **(13 June)** and Chiva **(13 July)**. On **12 September** his combined armies of North and Centre are outside Madrid with 16,000 troops, but Carlos shrinks from this opportunity, and defeat by Gen Espartero at Retuerta **(19th)** turns him north. Only 5,000 of his men return to Carlist territory, but Army of Centre in Maestrazgo gains extra troops and prestige. Exertions and costs of this campaign to both sides lead to stalemate in the north, and to growing disunity among Don Carlos's generals, between diehards ('Apostolics') and pragmatists ('Transactionists').

1838:

26 Jan Cabrera's Army of Centre takes Morella; thereafter he constructs defences around his territory, held by regularized forces.

March–April Last major Carlist expedition, by Count Negri with large Castilian force, is defeated by Espartero at Valladolid **(27 April)**.

1 May Espartero appointed captain-general of Liberal armies.

22 June Espartero defeats Guergué at Peñacerrada.

July Cabrera repels attempt to retake Morella.

1 October Cabrera's greatest victory: defeats Liberal Gen Pardiñaras in pitched battle at Maella.

1839:

February Factional struggle between northern Carlist leaders. Gen Maroto executes *apostolicos*, is dismissed by Don Carlos, but restored on insistence of army. Maroto begins secret negotiations with Liberals.

26 August Espartero and Maroto sign Armistice of Vergara; remnant of Army of North capitulates.

14 September Don Carlos flees to France. Thereafter Espartero's troops advance gradually against Army of Centre, taking successive towns.

1840:

19–30 May Espartero successfully besieges Morella, with 20,000 men and strong siege train.

6 July Cabrera retreats into France, with 8,000 of his own men and 5,000 Catalonians. End of First Carlist War; the Second will break out in 1848.

General Baldomero Espartero, captain-general of the Liberal forces from May 1838. Of humble birth, he joined the Spanish army as a young volunteer during the war against Napoleon, rising to the rank of general by his great abilities (as demonstrated in South American campaigns). In the Carlist War he reorganized the Liberal Army after the defeats of the early years, decisively improving its training, discipline, efficiency and morale. By the end of the conflict Espartero was the real master of Spain: he was Regent in 1840–43, and ruled the country again in 1854–56.

THE LIBERAL ARMY

The Spanish Army of 1833 was not particularly strong, and suffered from structural problems in the cavalry and the technical corps, but during the First Carlist War it notably expanded its size and improved its standards.

The new army of 1814 had been influenced by both the guerrilla tradition of 'the nation in arms', and by the professional doctrines of the French and British armies. The rankers were less subservient than before, and the officer corps came from a wider spectrum of society than the old aristocracy. Consequently, during 1814–33 the army was broadly favourable to the Liberals, though with some notable exceptions (such as the Royal Guard). In 1823, however, it was easily defeated by the French. Thereafter the king ordered the creation of a 'parallel army' by the establishment of the *Voluntarios Realistas* (see below, 'The Carlist Armies'). This paramilitary organization, raised nationally, was intended to provide both a counterbalance against the regulars' Liberal sympathies, and a nucleus for the formation of royalist insurgent groups in case of renewed revolution.

Thereafter the army was heavily purged of all elements (especially officers) suspected of subversive ideas – both Liberals, *and* ultra-conservatives. The latter included Tomás de Zumalacárregui and many other future Carlist officers, who were deprived of their commands. When the conflict started in 1833 all units of the regular army remained loyal to Maria Christina; during the war a good many individuals crossed over to the Carlists or deserted, but never en masse.

ORGANIZATION
The Liberal Army of 1833 was organized according to the Royal Decree of 31 May 1828, and numbered some 115,000 men raised by conscription.

Grenadiers (centre) and Cazadores (left & right) of the Provincial 2nd Division of the Royal Guard. This shows the 1833 uniforms, before the removal of the braids across the front of the coatee (compare with Plate A3). The two Provincial regiments of grenadiers differed from those of the 1st Division in wearing yellow rather than white braid. The Guard Cazadores' uniform was as follows: Black shako with yellow top band, pompon and plume, red cockade, and brass plate. Dark blue coatee with red collar, cuff flaps, turnbacks and piping; yellow epaulettes, yellow braiding on collar, cuffs and front. Dark blue trousers with red stripe in winter, plain white in summer; black or white gaiters, black shoes.

Royal Guard

Unlike many foreign household troops, the Spanish Royal Guard was a large and effective combat force numbering 15,000 elite soldiers. After having lost control of his army for three years, in 1824 Ferdinand VII transformed the Royal Guard into a strong and loyal private army of horse, foot and guns. Despite a tendency to play politics (e.g. in August 1836), the Royal Guard would prove to be a solid asset for the Liberals; at the beginning of the war it was the largest body of effective troops able to confront the Carlists, and thus saw a great deal of action while the line regiments were being brought up to standard. Its units did not fight as a separate division, but were brigaded with line regiments to stiffen the various Liberal field armies.

The Royal Guard was divided into the *Guardia Real Interior* and *Guardia Real Exterior*; the former were small ceremonial units attending the king, while the latter were the field troops. The 'Interior Royal Guard' was composed of two units: the mounted bodyguards of the *Guardias de la Real Persona*, and the foot halberdiers of the *Reales Guardias de Alabarderos*. The former had four 126-strong mounted squadrons, two of light cavalry and two of mounted grenadiers; the latter, after reorganization in 1836, had 16 captains and 128 sergeant halberdiers.

The 'Exterior Royal Guard' was organized in three large, well-trained divisions with excellent equipment. The 1st Division consisted of 4 regiments of grenadiers. The 2nd Div had 2 regiments each of grenadiers and *cazadores* (light infantry); these were known as the *Guardia Real Provincial* because their companies had originally been drawn, in 1824, from the Provincial militia (see below). The infantry regiments had 3 battalions each of 8 companies; in the grenadiers units these were all grenadiers, and in the regiments of cazadores they were all light infantry.

The 3rd Div provided the Guard cavalry: a brigade each of line and light cavalry, and a detached squadron of horse artillery. The Line Bde had a regiment each of cuirassiers and mounted grenadiers, the Light Bde a regiment each of lancers and mounted chasseurs. The cavalry regiments each had 3 service squadrons of 2 companies, plus a depot squadron. In 1828 a company of carbine-armed *tiradores* was added to each cavalry unit except the Mounted Chasseurs, which received one only during the war. In 1833 the Horse Artillery Sqn had 3 four-gun batteries: one battery *a caballo* (with both gunners and drivers mounted), and two *montadas* (with the gunners riding on limbers). In 1835 the squadron was transformed into a brigade by the addition of a fourth (*montado*) battery. During the war the 4 mounted regiments of the Royal Guard in fact all performed more or less the same light-cavalry functions; the nature of the terrain and the chronic shortage of suitable horses obliged the high command to employ the heavy regiments, too, for scouting, patrolling and screening.

This elegant regular infantry officer wears a dark blue *bonnet de police* braided, piped and tasselled in silver; a dark blue coatee with silver epaulettes and a gilt gorget; and reinforced grey overalls.

Line infantry

At the outbreak of war the line infantry comprised 19 regiments, of which one, the *Fijo de Ceuta*, garrisoned the Moroccan city of that name, and was not numbered. The others were numbered 1–18; the first 14 and the Fijo de Ceuta had 3 battalions each, and those numbered 15–18 only 2, but these received 3rd Bns early in the war. (There were also 3 regiments of Swiss infantry, but these were already in the process of disbandment and played no part in the war.) Each line battalion had a depot company plus 8 active companies: 6 of fusiliers, 1 of grenadiers and 1 of cazadores. On campaign, grenadier and light companies from different battalions were frequently assembled to form special assault units. This organization remained more or less the same throughout the war, the only exception being the formation of 8 independent provisional battalions (numbered 1–8) during 1837–39. These were created with surplus conscripts from the depot companies of both line and light infantry regiments.

In addition to the regiments of the line, the army also included a certain number of **Provincial regiments** – second-line units with partial training (for just two hours on the first Sunday of each month) and equipment. This kind of militia had a long tradition in Spain, with the main peacetime task of providing cadres to garrison the provinces, to be transformed into an active reserve in time of war. However, the turmoil of Ferdinand's reign obliged the government to employ the Provincial regiments on a larger scale than originally planned. From 1824 they provided 43 single-battalion regiments (of which chosen companies were detached to form the Provincial regiments of the Royal Guard – see above). During 1834–39 the Provincial units were all fully mobilized, receiving new conscripts like any other regular regiment. They were expanded 'on paper' to a theoretical strength of 1,200 men each, although the average was actually around 500–700. Despite their handicaps, some Provincial regiments performed well enough during the conflict to earn conversion into regulars subsequently.

Light infantry

In 1833 the army included 6 *cazadores* regiments of light infantry, each of 2 battalions. The battalion structure was the same as in the line infantry, but with different company denominations: *cazadores* (equivalent to fusiliers), *carabineros* (equivalent to grenadiers), and *tiradores* (corresponding to the cazadores in line units). Despite their different uniforms and designations, the light regiments had the same weapons and equipment as the line. As the war progressed the government felt an increasing need for light infantry; line regiments were not best suited for the operations in the north, which were mainly conducted in the mountains,

Line infantry early in the war, the sitting soldier in winter trousers. At left, note the old-pattern long shako plume: white, and rising from a pompon in company colour. This soon proved impractical; at right is its shorter replacement, entirely in company colour.

so necessarily in open order. Consequently 3 new regiments of cazadores were formed: *Albuera* (November 1835), *Reina Gobernadora* (December 1835) and *Cazadores de Luchana* (September 1837).

Of these new units the Reina Gobernadora ('Queen Regent', in honour of Maria Christina, who was its honorary colonel) was a genuine elite. It had 3 battalions instead of 2, and its soldiers were armed with Baker rifles, so in that sense it was the only true 'light infantry' regiment in the army. The Cazadores de Luchana was initially created as a single battalion named *Guías del General* and formed with Carlist deserters. In May 1838 these 'General's Guides' were transformed into a regiment by the addition of a second battalion formed with conscripts, and renamed.

Cavalry

The cavalry was the branch with the most serious problems in 1833. Ferdinand VII had always distrusted this arm as particularly favouring the Liberals, and had disbanded various veteran units. The shortage of experienced horsemen resulting from these purges seriously limited the operational capabilities of the regular cavalry, which was unable to confront Carlist mounted units on equal terms for most of the war. The situation improved to some degree only during the second half of the conflict, thanks to positive reforms in training and discipline introduced by talented commanders such as the outstanding Diego de León of the Royal Guard Lancers and Princess's Hussars. The nature of the terrain over which most of the war was fought precluded the use of large cavalry formations, and squadrons from any given regiment were usually dispersed on detached service, even for years at a time. In addition, the Liberal cavalry always suffered from a shortage of good remounts. Its main wartime tasks were scouting, convoy escort, and guarding against incursions by Carlist guerrillas.

In 1833 the cavalry included 5 numbered regiments of line (heavy) cavalry and 7 of light horse, although – as in the infantry – there was little practical difference between them. Each regiment had 4 squadrons, each divided into 2 companies, and extra officers so that in wartime it could rapidly be expanded to 6 squadrons; in the event, however, these 5th and 6th Sqns were never formed, for lack of recruits. By a reorganization of 16 November 1835 the squadrons of each regiment were divided between 3 on active service and a depot squadron to train conscripts. In March 1838 all line and light cavalry regiments received an extra company of tiradores armed with carbines.

In addition to these 12 numbered regiments, the cavalry also included the elite *Húsares de la Princesa* – named for the Infant Queen Isabella. This was formed on 16 March 1833, with experienced officers selected on the basis of their loyalty. Initially providing a ceremonial guard of honour, the 'Princess's Hussars' were soon deployed in the field, and would become the army's best cavalry unit. Its internal organization was conventional, including the incorporation of a carbine company in 1838.

Finally, there was also an independent light squadron forming part of the capital's garrison; this 'Madrid Sqn' initially had 2 companies, but received a third in March 1838. A new light horse regiment, the *Guías del General del Ejército del Norte*, was also created that month; these 'Guides of the General of the Northern Army' were formed from 3 squadrons of mounted *peseteros* (see below, 'Cristino volunteers'). Considered a provisional unit, it was not given a number.

Artillery

Artillery played a limited part in the First Carlist War. Many of the field forces deployed by the government either lacked guns entirely or reduced their number to a minimum, despite having well-trained gunners and competent officers. This tendency was partly due to the mountainous terrain, but mainly to a shortage of suitable draught animals. In most of the main theatre of operations only small mountain guns transported on mules could have been of real use, but the Liberal artillery mainly consisted of heavy field pieces. Additionally, the Carlist artillery did not represent a serious threat. In open-field battles the Carlists usually fought in open order, so there was little chance to use artillery against them effectively; the few sieges were the only occasions when the Liberal technical corps played a crucial role.

In 1833 the regular artillery had 3 foot regiments with 2 battalions each, the battalion having 3 companies/batteries (these terms being used interchangeably) and one train company. The foot regiments were based in the military districts of Valladolid, Sevilla and Barcelona. Two new regiments were raised in May 1835, based in Valencia and La Coruña districts. Two horse artillery squadrons, with 3 batteries each, were also based in Valladolid and Sevilla. In May 1835 this arm was increased from 6 to 12 batteries, structured in 3 brigades with 4 batteries each, the brigades being based in Valladolid, Valencia and Sevilla. Apparently only one of these brigades was *a caballo*, the other two being *montadas*. A fourth brigade of horse artillery would be added in 1840.

From the first months of the war the need for light mountain batteries was clear, but their formation proved to be difficult and time-consuming. By 1838 there were 2 new brigades, each with 6 batteries/companies of mule-pack mountain guns; the batteries had 8 howitzers each, for a total of 96. These two brigades (classed as *a lomo*, 'on animal-back') were based in the Valladolid and Barcelona districts.

The Spanish artillery also included a certain number of fixed garrison units, organized into 6 brigades with 2 companies each; the departments of Valladolid, Barcelona and Sevilla each had 2 of these static brigades. In addition to all the above, each of the five military districts of the country had a company of artillery workers. In July 1839 a new company of armourers was formed, based in Sevilla.

Engineers

The Royal Corps of Engineers consisted of a single regiment, having 2 battalions with 7 companies each. Of these companies 5 were of sappers, 1 of miners and 1 of pontoniers. In November 1835 company strength was increased to 150 men, but otherwise the organization remained unchanged. The Engineers played an important role, especially during the first phase of the war, when they had to restore most of the regular

Line infantry officer wearing unregulated campaign dress. His shako has a silver top band, pompon and tuft, a red cockade, brass plate and chinscales (presumably gilt). The dark blue coatee shows red collar patches (he is probably from a grenadier company), and note the gilt gorget. Both the 'booted' overalls and the greatcoat are grey, the latter with a silver epaulette and contre-epaulette.

army's neglected fortifications. They were also fundamental to the Liberals' successes in the few siege operations, showing the technical superiority of regulars in this kind of warfare. In addition, throughout the conflict they built a series of defensive lines and new fortifications that seriously limited the Carlists' offensives and smaller raids.

Naval troops

On 7 January 1827 the Spanish naval infantry and artillery were reorganized into a single *Brigada Real de Marina* having 3 large battalions, each of 24 officers and 1,344 men in 6 companies (without elite companies), reduced to 2 battalions on 18 May 1830. In 1833 the brigade was renamed the Royal Corps of Naval Artillery. In 1836, 3 new battalions were raised, bringing the total to 5, each still with 6 companies. In 1839 the Corps was redesignated yet again, as the Naval Infantry and Artillery Corps; the 1st and 2nd Bns were artillery, the 3rd–5th infantry. Detached companies of these marines usually served on warships, but during the war several contingents served on land as normal line infantry. After the subdivision of 1839 the artillery remained in coastal garrisons, while the infantry battalions were deployed with the field army.

Militia

The constitution of 1812 was the first official document that recognized all Spanish citizens fighting for the freedom of their country from France as a *milicia nacional,* thus starting a tradition of citizen military activity that was to last for most of the 19th century. In 1814, shortly before King Ferdinand's restoration, the National Militia was established as an auxiliary force independent from the regular army, comprising both

Liberal Army mounted units: (from left to right), Hussars, Line Cavalry, Horse Artillery, Light Cavalry (background), and Horse Artillery of the Royal Guard. For colours, compare the Hussar with Plate D2, but this man wears the new, shorter 1835 shako. For the Line trooper, see Plate C1. The horse gunner wears the same colours as Plate D1, with cavalry equipment; the shako cords were often removed on campaign.
For the Light Cavalryman see Plate C3, and for the Royal Guard horse gunner, Plate A4.

infantry and cavalry units. Men between the ages of 30 and 50 were required to serve, at a ratio of 30 men from each 1,300 inhabitants, with officers chosen locally by their own men. Because of its semi-democratic organization and its separation from the regular army, the National Militia was seen as a politicized force, the armed wing of the Liberals: for these reasons its abolition was one of Ferdinand's first acts upon his return. During 1820–23 ('the Three Liberal Years') it was re-established in two branches: the Volunteer National Militia and the Active National Militia were intended as, respectively, a sedentary reserve and garrison force, and an auxiliary force for the regular army. Many units, particularly in major cities, proved their worth during the French invasion of 1823, which the militia generally resisted with more determination than the regulars.

With Ferdinand's second restoration in 1823 the militia was again disbanded, and the king ordered the creation of the Royal Volunteers as a substitute (see below, 'The Carlist Armies'). In 1833, with the death of Ferdinand and the return of the Liberals, the militia was re-formed under the name Volunteers of Isabella II – changed to Urban Militia in 1834; then to National Guard; and finally, in 1835, to National Militia. During the conflict it played only a secondary role as a part-time local defence force, but some units were quite important in countering minor Carlist raids. Militia cavalry and artillery units were rare; the infantry were organized into battalions generally having 6-10 companies (some even including elite 'flank' companies).

Paramilitary units

The Spanish civil police (*Intendencia General de Policía*) were aided by two paramilitary organizations, very similar to the Napoleonic Gendarmerie: the *Carabineros de Costas y Fronteras*, and in Catalonia the *Mossos d'Esquadra*.

The Carabineers were established on 9 March 1829 to protect the coasts and frontiers, targeting smuggling and tax fraud, but very soon began operating throughout the country to support the police in putting down local banditry. Having military training and equipment, the Carabineers were of great help to the regular army during the First Carlist War. In 1833 they had a total of 9,282 men in foot and mounted units divided into 12 commands located across Spain; in that same year they changed their name to *Carabineros de la Real Hacienda*. This corps was fundamental to the Madrid government's success in keeping control of most of the provinces during the first phase of Carlist risings.

Catalonia had its own long-standing paramilitary police force, the *Mossos d'Esquadra* (literally meaning 'the Lads of the Squads'). Speaking Catalan, and familiar with their territory, these strong supporters of the monarchy played an important role against Carlist insurgents. Their renown was such that even the Carlists of Catalonia and Aragon formed two small units wearing the same uniforms as the royalist force, which acted as escorts for Carlist commanders.

'Cristino' volunteers

In addition to the regulars, militia and gendarmes, the Liberal government employed units of volunteers who were known as *'peseteros'* from their daily pay of one peseta (a lot more than the regulars received).

Fusilier from the Urban Militia of Madrid. For colours compare with Plate D3, but this man has yellow centre-company epaulettes.

Volunteer of the Chappelgorris batallion, wearing the 'regular' uniform issued after they joined Gen Espartero's army. See plate E2.

In the early months of the war, when the regular army was in no condition to defend the provinces bordering Carlist territories, local citizens started to form irregular units. As time passed the government regularized these *tropas francas* and provided weapons and equipment. The Peseteros were particularly hated by the Carlists, because many of them were either 'Cristinos' who had escaped from Carlist territory, or Carlist deserters (who were rarely accepted into the Liberal regular army). Familiar with Carlist tactics and territory, the Peseteros adopted the same guerrilla methods and light equipment. Because of their black or dark green uniforms, they were generally called *'Los Negros'* by their enemies. With the ascendancy of Gen Espartero as commander-in-chief of the Liberal forces the Peseteros gradually declined in importance, and by the end of the war they had almost disappeared.

The most famous unit of volunteers formed during the war was the *'Chapelgorris'* (in the Basque language, 'Red Caps', from their adoption of the red Carlist *boina* headgear). Raised in the Basque provinces of Alava, Guipúzcoa and Vizcaya, these volunteers formed a battalion of 400–500 men that soon became famous for both its valour and its lack of discipline. Because of their proven prowess the 'Red Caps' were the only formed unit of Peseteros incorporated into the regular army by Gen Espartero. They included a certain number of foreigners, mostly rebel deserters; for this reason the Chapelgorris were particularly hated by the Carlists, who usually tortured and killed any they captured. In 1836 the battalion was permanently attached to the British Auxiliary Legion, receiving new red uniforms. According to British observers, the Chapelgorris chose their own officers and showed little respect to any regular soldier. Using the same equipment as the Carlists, they were described as an excellent light infantry unit of hard fighters, but always inclined to plundering.

FOREIGN ALLIES

British Auxiliary Legion

British involvement in the Peninsular War (1808–14) had naturally fostered strong links with the Iberian countries. In the first half of the 19th century British governments gave financial and diplomatic support to liberal movements across Europe, for both ideological and commercial motives, and during the Portuguese Liberal Wars (1828–34) British naval forces openly supported Dom Pedro's liberals. Several units of adventurers and mercenaries also participated, finally growing into an entire British brigade of foot and horse.

From November 1833 the British prime minister, Lord Palmerston, ordered the Royal Navy to blockade the Carlist-held coasts of northern Spain, and as the war progressed this naval involvement became ever more direct and significant. In June 1835, at a time of difficulties for Maria Christina's army, the British decided to organize an Auxiliary Legion for her forces (its being paid by the Madrid government would allow Britain an element of deniability, even though London was bankrolling the Liberals). George De Lacy Evans was chosen as commander of this force, which was entirely composed of volunteers; recruiting proved quite easy, and by the beginning of July 1835 the first British contingents had landed in Spain.

By the end of October the completed British Auxiliary Legion could field 7,800 men (3,200 Englishmen, 1,800 Scotsmen and 2,800 Irishmen), formally enlisted into the Spanish Army but under British conditions of service. The Legion included 10 single-battalion line regiments, though only some of them had the standard British structure of 10 companies (8 of fusiliers, 1 of grenadiers and 1 of light infantry); the others had 8 companies like Spanish line battalions. Of the numbered regiments, the 1st–4th were English, the 5th, 6th and 8th Scottish, and the 7th, 9th and 10th Irish. In addition the Legion included a Rifle Regt with 6 companies; 2 regiments of lancers (the 1st English, the 2nd Irish); and a field battery with two guns and two howitzers. Once in Spain, a small Corps of Sappers & Miners was formed with personnel drawn from the various units. High rates of sickness in winter 1835–36 forced the disbandment of the 2nd and 5th Bns, and on 5 May 1836 the Legion was divided into 3 brigades – English, Irish and Scottish – and the Scottish Bde also incorporated the 'Chapelgorris' battalion (see above). From time to time, according to operational needs, some regular contingents of Royal Marines, Royal Artillery and Royal Engineers were also temporarily attached to the Legion, whcih held positions on the north coast around San Sebastián.

FAR LEFT
Line infantry officer of the British Auxiliary Legion. The shako is black, with a red pompon and gilt brass furniture. Officers dressed very simply on campaign; the dark blue frock coat has brass buttons, and was always worn with the officers' crimson waist sash (just visible here), knotted on the left with long hanging tassels. The left contre-epaulette balanced by a fringed right epaulette traditionally identified a battalion adjutant. His trousers are shown as dark grey-blue with red seam-piping.

While the British Legion's commander, George De Lacy Evans, was a veteran of India, the Peninsula, the War of 1812 and Waterloo (and would survive to command a division in the Crimea), very few of his officers or men had combat experience. The youngest Peninsula veteran in the ranks would anyway have been approaching 40 years old.

LEFT
This line infantryman of the British Auxiliary Legion is depicted wearing a light blue peakless forage cap; this is of the banded, broad-crowned shape first ordered in 1829 and still illustrated in the early 1840s, despite the first appearance of the 'pork-pie' or Kilmarnock cap in the mid-1830s. His coatee is red, with yellow collar, cuffs, shoulder straps and braid on the wings – taken together with the grenade motif on his light blue canteen, these identify him as from a grenadier company. His slightly ragged trousers are dark grey, his leather equipment white, and his knapsack black. For further details, see commentary to Plate E1.

During the battle of Oriamendi (16 March 1837), a severe defeat for the Liberals, the British Legion suffered very high casualties, leading to a general reorganization of the line infantry. The survivors, about 3,300 strong, were assembled in 6 battalions, of which 2 were English, 2 Scottish, 1 Irish, and the last the Rifle unit.

The British Legion had been enlisted for just two years' service, during which it mainly operated from a base at San Sebastián (except for the 2nd Lancer Regt, which campaigned further afield with the Liberal forces). On 10 June 1837 the period of service ended and the Legion was disbanded; however, about 1,700 men wished to continue serving, so on the same date a 'Second Legion' was established, divided into 3 infantry battalions (Scottish, Irish, and Rifle), a regiment of lancers, and artillery and sapper elements. This new formation was short-lived, however, and was itself disbanded on 8 December 1837. Yet again, a certain number of soldiers chose to remain in Spain: about 400 were reorganized on 1 March 1838 into a new British Auxiliary Brigade, consisting of just a lancer regiment and an artillery battery (inherited from the Second Legion, with 4 light brass guns and 2 howitzers).

While the British contribution to the Liberal cause was quite significant in terms of men, the determining factors were Britain's continuing supplies of weapons and financial credit: 50 artillery pieces, 350,000 muskets, 3 million cartridges, and an indefinite amount in bank loans.

French Foreign Legion

Like Britain, France had strong political and economic interests in supporting Maria Christina's government, but also wanted to avoid a direct involvement of their regular forces in Spain. For this reason they simply transferred their entire recently-raised Foreign Legion from Algeria into the Spanish Army, though serving under its own officers. In August 1835 the Legion, commanded by Col Bernelle, disembarked at Tarragona in Catalonia with around 4,000 men organized into 6 infantry battalions, each having 6 companies of fusiliers and 2 elite companies. After several hard actions and a winter spent around Pamplona, in March 1836 Bernelle began to form, from within the Legion's ranks, three squadrons of Polish lancers and a mountain howitzer battery; the expense was met by diverting the men's back pay. During summer 1836 a 7th Bn arrived from France as reinforcement. In February 1837 the new commander, Col Conrad, reduced the number of battalions to 3, but later their elite companies were assembled to re-form a 4th Battalion.

Hard fighting in March again reduced the Foreign Legion to just 2 battalions. During this same period the Carlists formed a unit of, at its peak, 850 men known as the 'Argelino' (Algerian) Bn, with Legion deserters. Reduced to a single battalion after the battle of Huesca on 24 May 1837 while resisting the Carlist 'Royal Expedition', on 1 June the Legion was finally destroyed at Barbastro in a bloody clash against the renegades of the Argelino Bn (which was itself annihilated). Over the following month the lancers and gunners were incorporated into Spanish regular units; neglected thereafter, the Foreign Legion was finally disbanded on 8 December 1838, and about 500 survivors returned to France. It had often fought hard and effectively, but since it was only rarely supplied or paid, its potential was largely wasted.[1]

---

1   For further details of this deployment, see MAA 509, *French Foreign Legion 1831-1871*.

France also supported the Liberal cause with money and weapons, as well as contributing to the naval blockade and preventing military equipment being sent to the Carlists across the Pyrenees.

Portuguese Auxiliary Division

At the end of the wars fought in Portugal during 1828–34 the liberals led by Dom Pedro defeated King Miguel's conservatives, partly due to British and French support. Until Ferdinand VII's death Spain had been aiding Miguel, and after the outbreak of the First Carlist War in 1833 Spain's Don Carlos continued to support the Portuguese conservatives, while Maria Christina's new government planned a military intervention to help the Portuguese liberals. After his victory, the grateful Dom Pedro sent an expeditionary force to support the Queen Regent.

This Portuguese Auxiliary Division consisted of three brigades totalling 6,750 men (6,000 foot and 750 horse), and included some of the best units from the recently reformed Portuguese Army. The division's order of battle upon its arrival in Spain in November 1835 was as follows:

1st Brigade: 1st Bn/ 3rd Line Inf Regt; 1st Bn/ 3rd Light Inf (Caçadores) Regt; mountain artillery battery; detachment from Sapper Bn.

Portuguese infantry officers, from Knötel's *Uniformkunde.* The M1834 shako for the line; had brass (or gilt) furniture, the national cockade, and a plume in company colour (red, light blue, and green, for grenadiers, centre, and light companies respectively). New double-breasted dark blue coatees with two close-set rows of buttons had epaulettes in company colours for rankers. The piping to collar, cuffs and cuff flaps was white for all regiments, but these facings were of regimental colours: (1st Line) scarlet collar and cuff flaps, dark blue cuffs; (3rd Line) white collar and cuff flaps, dark blue cuffs; (6th Line) yellow collar and cuff flaps, dark blue cuffs; (9th Line) white collar and cuffs, dark blue cuff flaps; and (10th Line) light blue collar and cuffs, dark blue cuff flaps. Trousers were grey. Officers wore gold epaulettes and a red waist sash; an alternative frock coat service dress (far left) included a peaked forage cap with a band in regimental collar colour.
(Centre) Officer of *Caçadores* light infantry; note the tapered shako with green tuft, brown uniform with black plastrons, and partly metallic epaulettes. The collar, cuffs and cuff flaps were in regimental colours – see under Plate E4.

Portuguese cavalry officers, from Knötel's *Uniformkunde:* 3rd Mounted Chasseurs (left) and 2nd Lancers. The former had a black bell-topped shako with the national cockade, and a brass top band, plate and chinscales (presumably gilded for officers); the plume was red. The lancers had a red *czapska* with gilt furniture, gold cords and lines, and a black falling plume. Both units wore dark blue double-breasted coatees with collar and cuffs in regimental colours, the former with two gold lace bars, and gilt shoulder scales. The 3rd Regt had collar and cuffs in white, the 2nd Regt in crimson, both with yellow cuff piping. The trousers were grey with red stripes and piping.

2nd Brigade: 1st Bn/ 1st Line Inf Regt; 1st Bn/ 10th Line Inf Regt; 2 sqns/ 2nd Cav Regt (Lancers); horse artillery battery; detachment from Sapper Bn.

3rd Brigade: 1st Bn/ 6th Line Inf Regt; 1st Bn/ 9th Line Inf Regt; 1st Bn/ 4th Light Inf Regt; 2 sqns/ 3rd Cav Regt (Mounted Chasseurs); detachment from Sapper Bn.

On 2 February 1836 the division was reorganized into two 'columns' due to the casualties and desertions suffered. The 1st Column included the infantry battalions from the 3rd, 6th and 10th Line and the 4th Caçadores, and the squadrons from the 3rd Cavalry; the 2nd Column had the battalions from the 1st and 9th Line and the 3rd Caçadores, and the squadrons from the 2nd Cavalry. During most of its time in Spain the Portuguese Division acted in defence against Carlist thrusts into the provinces bordering Portugal. In August 1837, after suffering a defeat at Zambana, one of the two columns mutinied and marched back to Portugal; the other, ordered to pursue the mutineers, soon abandoned Spain too.

In addition to the Auxiliary Division composed of regular soldiers, the Portuguese government also sent an independent **Auxiliary Brigade** of two foreign battalions: the Grenadiers of Oporto (993 men, mostly British) and the Caçadores of Oporto (1,706 men, mostly Belgian). These were adventurers left over from various foreign mercenary units that Dom Pedro had been obliged to recruit early in his own civil war, when most of the Portuguese regular army had sided with King Miguel I.

WEAPONS

In 1814 the standard infantry weapon in Spain was the British flintlock 'Brown Bess' (Short Land Pattern, locally known as the 'Tower' musket). Attempts to produce a new 'national' musket were unsuccessful until the appearance of the M1828, one of the last and best flintlocks produced in Europe. By 1833, however, the numbers manufactured were still insufficient to equip more than a few units, and when the war broke out most regulars were still armed with the Brown Bess or the French M1777.

During the war Britain sold Spain approximately 350,000 more surplus muskets. The predominance of British weapons led to ammunition problems, since they took a larger ball than the Spanish muskets (0.75in to 0.69 inch). For this reason, from 1836 the Spanish government launched production of a new M1836 (a modified M1828) in the British calibre, which would be the Spanish infantry's last flintlock weapon. The light infantry had the same weapons as the line, apart from the elite Reina Gobernadora Regt equipped with Baker rifles. Liberal infantrymen also had local copies of the French M1816 *sabre-briquet*.

In 1833 the line (heavy) cavalry were equipped with the straight M1815 sword copied from that of Napoleon's cuirassiers; similarly, the light horse had the curved M1822 sabre copied from the French Napoleonic weapon, though both swords appeared in a number of slightly variant forms. The mounted units of the Royal Guard used these same weapons. However, surplus French and British weapons were also seen, including the British M1796 light cavalry sabre.

In 1833 both line and light cavalry were also equipped with flintlock carbines, either Spanish M1815 or M1831 models or surplus British or French weapons. The Hussars, formed shortly before the war, carried M1822 sabres and carbines. Of the Royal Guard cavalry, only the Mounted Grenadiers and Mounted Chasseurs had carbines for all troopers, the Cuirassiers and Lancers having carbines only for the company of *tiradores* that had been added to each regiment in 1828.

1835–36 saw a revolution, with the introduction of the lance as the cavalry's main weapon. Early in the conflict the Queen Regent's cavalry had experienced serious difficulties when confronting excellent Carlist light horse units, who lacked carbines but employed the lance with impressive skill. It was therefore decided to give lances to the entire cavalry, who were no longer to use carbines. (One is forced to wonder how long it took to retrain the troopers to effectively handle the lance, a notoriously tricky weapon.) In 1836 a new model of cavalry carbine, known as the M1836 and deriving from the equivalent infantry musket, started production, but because of the adoption of the lance its distribution was limited. Finally, in 1839, the first percussion weapon was officially adopted, but this M1839 carbine saw very limited service before the end of the war. The paramilitary Carabineers had infantry muskets and bayonets when on foot, and the same M1822 sabres and flintlock carbines as the light cavalry when mounted.

Royal Guard and line horse artillerymen were armed with M1822 light cavalry sabres, while foot gunners generally had shorter versions of the various infantry muskets. In addition, at least in theory, foot gunners had a local copy of the French M1831 *sabre-glaive* or '*coupe-choux*' known as the Machete Modelo 1834. As an alternative, in 1836 they received a new M1836 short sword specifically designed for them, and mounted and mountain gunners received a new M1836 flintlock musketoon.

The artillery's guns were of bronze and based on the French Gribeauval system, which had been introduced into Spain in 1783. Standard pieces included 24-, 16-, 12- (long and short), 8- (long and short) and 4-pounder guns, and 9- or 7-pdr howitzers. In the first campaigns short 8-pdr guns and 7-pdr howitzers were employed as mountain artillery; by the end of the war, however, the standard mountain gun had become a short, rechambered 5-pdr howitzer. Contemporary British models of gun carriage and boxed limber began to be used from 1833. The Liberals also acquired from Britain a certain number of Congreve rockets.

The line infantry of the British Auxiliary Legion carried the Brown Bess, and the Rifle Regt the Baker rifle. The lancers had British M1822 light cavalry sabres and lances. The artillery of the 'First' Legion consisted of 2x 6-pdr guns and 2x 12-pdr howitzers; that of the 'Second', 4x 6-pdr guns and 2x 12-pdr howitzers. Some Congreve rockets were also used. The French Foreign Legion was armed with French M1822 muskets and M1831 'cabbage-cutters' or older *sabre-briquets*. The lancers had French An XI light cavalry sabres, while the small artillery battery had short 5-pdr mountain howitzers. The Portuguese Division's infantry, both fusiliers and caçadores, were all armed with the Brown Bess. The light cavalry had local copies of the French M1822 sabre, or the British M1796.

THE CARLIST ARMIES

The Spanish regulars' loyalty to the throne on the outbreak of war was not mirrored by the *Voluntarios Realistas*, which had been formed in June 1823 when King Ferdinand regained control of the armed forces after three years of Liberal rule. During the French invasion of that year thousands of conservatives in the northern provinces had formed bands of *guerrilleros* to support Ferdinand and his French allies against the Liberal forces, and these later formed the basis of the king's replacement for the disbanded Liberal militia. By 1826 these 'Royal Volunteers' numbered some 200,000 men, organized into 486 infantry battalions, 52 cavalry squadrons, 20 artillery companies and several sapper companies. Like the former militia, only about half had uniforms and proper weapons; nevertheless, when they defied Madrid's order disbanding them in the first convulsive weeks of the conflict, and passed en masse into Don Carlos's service, they provided a strong nucleus for the military units that he at once began to form.

CARLIST ARMY OF THE NORTH

The Army of the North was the most regular of the three armies organized by Don Carlos's supporters, and it was remarkable that such an effective force could be raised from the relatively small populations of Navarre and the Basque provinces. This was only possible because of their widespread enthusiasm for his cause, harnessed by the military talents of Tomás de Zumalacárregui. The commander of the northern forces succeeded in forming scattered groups of insurgents into a functioning army in a matter of months. By June 1834 the Army of the North numbered some 15,000 men, and at its peak in January 1837 it mustered 35,000.

The first nucleus consisted of the Voluntarios Realistas of Navarre and the Basque provinces (Alava, Guipúzcoa and Vizcaya), who, unlike those elsewhere, had not already been disarmed by the government. To these were added a large number of volunteers who flocked to join the initial guerrilla bands when Don Carlos was proclaimed king. The Carlist armies would be composed of volunteers for most of the conflict: although attrition forced the Northern Army to introduce conscription during 1837 in the provinces it controlled, this was generally ineffective. Other sources of manpower were deserters from the Liberal forces and pressed prisoners, but these were never very significant.

During the early months of 1834 Zumalacárregui began creating a hard core of versatile infantry units. The men were mostly highlanders with great physical resilience, accustomed to the harsh terrain of the northern provinces and with a natural talent for guerrilla tactics. The Carlists were obliged to fight a guerrilla war while building their army during the first half of the year, and this light infantry was capable of covering great distances at remarkable speed (reportedly, on occasion, up to 60 miles in 24 hours), allowing Zumalacárregui to misdirect his opponents by feints and to launch surprise attacks. He sometimes

achieved successes over the dispersed Liberal armies at odds of 4:1 or even 6:1 against, and even when he had to make tactical withdrawals he often inflicted heavy casualties and evaded pursuit. Gradually, however, he succeeded in making his army adaptable enough to confront regulars in pitched battle, fighting in column, line and square as well as in skirmish order (as was proved at Salvatierra in October 1834, and Ormáiztegui and Segura in January 1835).

Lacking permanent bases and always on the move, the army trained while it marched. When launching expeditions into Liberal territory the Carlists always aimed to attract more volunteers en route, and for this reason columns included extra cadres to organize them immediately; large numbers of Castilians were enlisted in this way. Discipline was harsh, and the death penalty was frequently applied.

Infantry

Zumalacárregui formed his infantry in independent battalions, averaging 600–800 men organized conventionally in 8 companies (6 of fusiliers and 2 flank companies). On paper, each company was to number 80 men and each battalion 640. Two elite 'Guides' battalions combed out the best men from other units for additional training; initially they were employed for special operations, but from 1836 reverted to normal infantry service.

Carlist officers generally dressed like their men, being usually distinguishable only by their swords and gold or silver epaulettes.
(Left) Red *boina* with white tassel; entirely dark green coatee (perhaps suggesting former regular service in the Cazadores?) with silver buttons and epaulettes, and grey trousers.
(Right) Fur- or fleece-lined *zamarra*, fastened with toggles and loops like a pelisse; this brown or black jacket, which could be worn over or instead of a frock coat, was particularly popular, not least because it was favoured by Gen Zumalacárregui. In this case it is dark brown, and is worn with a white-tasselled red *boina*, a grey shell jacket piped red at the collar, leather-reinforced overalls, and a red waist sash.

This rather naive drawing does accurately show the characteristic light infantry equipment that allowed great mobility in mountainous terrain: the white canvas *saco-morral* rigged as a knapsack, the *canana* belly pouch, and the light *alpargatas* shoes tied on with thongs. (Left) The short jacket is probably of civilian origin, like the striped blanket which can be used as a poncho. (Centre & right) The typical double-breasted greatcoats are shown with the collar either standing or folded open. Northern Army greatcoats were usually made of grey cloth obtained from southern France; while the blockade stopped most weapons, other supplies did get across the Pyrenees. Note (centre) the unstiffened *boina* worn over a patterned bandana tied around the head, and (right) the musket drawn without barrel bands, so probably a 'Brown Bess'.

The Guides of Navarre were probably the best infantry unit in the Northern Army. They originally wore a red beret with a yellow roundel and black tassel; a grey coatee with brass buttons and a yellow collar, turnbacks, and bands of braid across the chest; red trousers (here, white for summer); and a grey mantle. In 1836 they changed to a blue shell jacket faced with red, and grey trousers.

The battalion's flag (centre) bearing a white death's-head on black is a reminder that both sides in this war often behaved brutally. In January 1834 Don Carlos's 'penal law' sanctioned the shooting of prisoners. In April 1835 a British diplomat persuaded Zumalacárregui and Gen Valdés to sign the Eliot Convention, agreeing to renounce this practice, but how widely it was honoured is open to doubt. It never applied outside the northern theatre, and in June 1835 Don Carlos's Durango Decree explicitly denied its protection to the Liberals' British and French allies.

Units were usually grouped into brigades of 3 battalions, and divisions of 6 to 8 battalions. At the time of Zumalacárregui's death in June 1835 the fully organized Army of the North had 35 battalions identified by their home provinces, although units from different provinces were frequently brigaded together. Their origins were:

Navarre, 12 line bns, 1 Guides bn; Alava, 5 line bns, 1 Guides bn; Guipúzcoa, 5 line bns; Vizcaya, 7 line bns; and Castile, 4 line battalions.

By 1837, at its peak of expansion, the army mustered 46 infantry battalions: from Navarre, 11 bns; Alava, 7 bns (of which the elite 5th Bn acted as Royal Guard for Don Carlos); Guipúzcoa, 8 bns; Vizcaya, 9 bns;

Castile, 4 bns; Aragon, 2 bns; Valencia, 2 bns; plus the battalions *Granaderos del Ejército, Argelino,* and *Voluntarios Distinguidos de Madrid.*

The Aragonese and Valencian units had been recruited by Gen Gómez during his remarkable expedition across most of the country in June–December 1836 (see Chronology). The Granaderos del Ejército was formed in 1836 with deserters from the regular Royal Guard, and this previous experience gave them an elite status. The Argelino Bn, as noted above, was formed with multi-national deserters from the French Foreign Legion. The men of Voluntarios Distinguidos de Madrid were volunteers from many parts of central and southern Spain, and notably from Madrid; they were not highly regarded, and were relegated to guarding the northern coast against incursions by the Royal Navy. In addition to the above, during the war the army also included three battalions from Cantabria; the

first was formed at the beginning of the conflict, the second in 1836 and the third in 1838. The Carlists also had the *Aduaneros,* a paramilitary customs-police corps guarding the French frontier and keeping order in territory under Carlist control.

In addition to Navarrese and Basques the Northern Army included many Castilians, who in 1837 represented about one-third of the total strength. These men either travelled north voluntarily from territory under Liberal control, or were recruited during the several Carlist incursions into Castile. Here Castilian infantry are depicted wearing a blue *boina* with a yellow roundel and white tassel, a grey double-breasted frock coat, and white trousers (red for winter). Note the 'regular'-looking small belly box, and what appear to be French Charleville M1777 muskets.

Castilian cavalry of the Army of the North; troopers from that province formed a number of usually short-lived provisional units raised for expeditions into Liberal-held territory, but Castilians made a longer-lasting contribution to Cabrera's Army of the Centre in Aragon. For colours, compare with Plate H3, except for the white summer trousers shown here.

The organization of the Navarrese and Basque battalions remained quite stable throughout the war, but the same could not be said of units from Castile. Apparently, a total of 12 Castilian battalions were raised during three Carlist expeditions into central Spain, this term being applied very broadly to any deserters, pressed prisoners, or volunteers taken up during the expeditions into Liberal-held provinces (and even to a unit of deserters from the Portuguese Auxiliary Division – see below). Consequently, these units – other than the original nucleus of 4 battalions – were usually short-lived.

The *Tropas de la Casa Real* ('Troops of the Royal House') were two small units formed by Don Carlos to bolster his royal dignity. The initial 'Halberdiers of the Royal Honour Guard' numbered 100 young local aristocrats who were actually armed with Baker rifles: 20 from each of the three Basque provinces, and 40 from Navarre. Later renamed the 'Honour Guard of Infantry', this company acted both as a bodyguard and a sort of military academy: on leaving, guardsmen were promoted to lieutenant and went to serve as infantry officers. There was also a similar carbine-armed 'Honour Guard of Cavalry' numbering just 25 volunteers, who acted as Don Carlos's personal mounted escort before being commissioned into the cavalry. To be admitted to either unit, a young nobleman had to have already served in the army for two years, and to have taken part in at least two actions. On 13 December 1837 the Household Troops were augmented by the creation of a new 30-strong *Escolta para el Estandarte de la Generalísima*. Also armed with carbines, this provided the ceremonial escort for the Carlists' sacred flag of the Virgin Mary.

Finally, the contribution to the Carlist cause made by Portuguese conservatives should be mentioned. Many of King Miguel's supporters did not accept the peace of 1834, and, wishing to continue the fight against the liberal cause, a number of them went to Spain to serve as volunteers for Don Carlos. They formed an independent Portuguese Company within the Army of the North, which was later expanded into a battalion with deserters from the Liberals' Portuguese Auxiliary Division.

Cavalry

Navarre and the Basque provinces were neither good horse-rearing country nor suitable terrain for cavalry operations, so Zumalacárregui gave little importance to raising mounted troops. However, these were valuable during the Carlist expeditions into central Spain. Almost all Carlist cavalrymen were lancers, and they rarely had carbines or pistols. Squadrons usually numbered between 90 and 120 men, and were organized according to their provinces. Navarre provided 4 squadrons, and the Basque provinces 1 each, of which the Alava Sqn was later named the 'Hussars of Arlában'.

For expeditions, provisional squadrons were sometimes formed with men from various units (several being designated as Castilian), but these were usually short-lived. The only stable units from that province were Merino's Lancers (see below, 'Carlist guerrillas'), and the 'Hussars of Ontoria'. The former were a semi-regular group of 400–500 led by the *guerrillero* veteran Jerónimo Merino. The Ontoria Hussars were probably the best trained and equipped mounted unit in the Northern Army. There was also a Cantabrian 'Squadron of the Princess', and the last Carlist

(continued on page 33)

EXTERIOR ROYAL GUARD
1: Trooper, Lancer Regt, 1836
2: Trooper, Cuirassier Regt, 1833
3: Grenadier, 1st Foot Grenadier Regt, 1833
4: Gunner, Horse Artillery Sqn, 1834

LIBERAL INFANTRY

1: Sergeant, Naval Infantry, 1834
2: Grenadier, Line Regt 'Rey', 1836
3: Sgt, light company, Cazadores Regt 'Reina Gobernadora', 1836
4: Cazador, Regt 'Cazadores del Rey', 1833

LIBERAL CAVALRY
1: Trooper, 3rd Line Cavalry Regt, 1833
2: Trooper, 4th Line Cavalry Regt, 1837
3: Trooper, 4th Light Cavalry Regt, 1834
4: Trooper, 2nd Light Cavalry Regt, 1838

LIBERAL ARMY

1: Gunner, 1st Foot Artillery Regt, 1833
2: Trooper, Regt 'Húsares de la Princesa', 1834
3: Soldier, light company, Milicia Urbana de Madrid, 1835
4: Mounted Carabinero, 1834

FOREIGN CONTINGENTS IN LIBERAL SERVICE
1: Lancer, British Auxiliary Legion, 1836
2: 'Chapelgorri', 1836
3: Lancer, French Foreign Legion, 1836
4: Caçador, Portuguese Auxiliary Div, 1835

CARLIST ARMY OF THE CENTRE, 1839
1: Grenadier, Tortosa Division
2: Infantryman, Valencia Division
3: Marine, *Compañías de Marina*
4: Artilleryman

CARLIST ELITE UNITS & IRREGULARS
1: Trooper, 'Ordenanzas del General' Sqn; Army of the Centre, 1839
2: Soldier, 'Miñones de Cabrera'; Army of the Centre, 1839
3: Soldier, 'Guías de Cabrera' Bn; Army of the Centre, 1839
4: Guerrillero, New Castile, 1837

CARLIST CAVALRY

1: Trooper, 'Húsares de Arlabán' Sqn; Army of the North, 1836
2: Lancer, Valencian cavalry; Army of the Centre, 1839
3: Lancer, Navarrese cavalry; Army of the North, 1835
4: Tirador, 'Lanceros de Tortosa' Regt; Army of the Centre, 1839

commander-in-chief, Gen Maroto, formed an escort named the 'Squadron of the Prince'. Finally, Zumalacárregui created an elite 'Squadron of Commanders and Officers' with surplus officers and ex-members of Ferdinand VII's bodyguard who had changed sides; apparently this unit was also known as the *Escuadrón de la Legitimidad*. Due to the chronic shortage of horses, for a while the army also included a 'Dismounted Squadron'.

Artillery and Engineers

At the beginning of the war the Carlist forces in the north had just 4 guns, and, despite great efforts by Zumalacárregui, their artillery remained insignificant until 1835. The initial 2 companies with mule-pack mountain guns were later organized into a battalion of 4 companies (reverting to 2 in 1837). The first, an elite company, was attached to the General Staff. In addition there were also 2 companies of garrison artillery, 2 of train, and 1 each of artillery workers and artillery cadets. Apparently most of the gunners were, of necessity, Liberal deserters.

The engineers initially had a single sapper company, and only in 1836 could they begin the formation (never completed) of a battalion of 5 companies (1 of these being cadets), plus 2 independent garrison companies. The engineers nevertheless had an important role during the few siege operations conducted by the Carlists, and constantly repaired the defensive fortifications protecting the areas the Northern Army controlled.

CARLIST ARMY OF THE CENTRE

This force developed completely differently from the 'royal' army created for Don Carlos in the north by Zumalacárregui, but despite humble beginnings it later became in one sense the most successful of the Carlist armies – in that it besieged, captured, and occupied, a major city and for some time held it against Liberal attack.

The same physical inaccessibility and local enthusiasm that the Carlists relied upon in the north also applied in Maestrazgo, a mountainous region of Aragon that soon became the base of this second major Carlist force, which would attract volunteers from all over Aragon and Valencia. From autumn 1833 there was intense and particularly ferocious fighting in Aragon between insurgents and local Liberal forces. While the fighting in the north became in some senses a conventional war, that in Aragon retained a distinctly guerrilla character. The Carlists in Maestrazgo initially dispersed into small groups to avoid direct confrontations with the regulars. The two most important bands were led by Ramón Cabrera and Manuel Carnicer; in December 1834 Cabrera travelled to Don Carlos's headquarters, and was granted command over the insurgents operating in Maestrazgo. Carnicer later marched 3,500 men north to join the main Carlist army, but his defeat at Mayals in April 1835, and his subsequent execution, left Cabrera without a rival.

Early in 1835 Cabrera began the process of transforming his guerrilla bands into regular units, but his forces grew more slowly than those in the north, and, while they would achieve important successes, they never reached the same level of discipline and effectiveness. Two handicaps were that the Royal Volunteers in Aragon had already been disarmed before the conflict started, and that the local Carlists never included many experienced ex-regular officers. The Army of the Centre remained

Don Carlos's Honour Guard of Cavalry are depicted with much more complete equipment than was issued to most Carlist troopers, including canteens, sabres, and carbines carried in saddle boots (all doubtless provided at his personal expense, since there were only 25 of them). They are illustrated wearing a red *boina* with yellow roundel and white tassel; a dark blue coatee with red collar, cuffs, turnbacks and piping; a red leather crossbelt and ammunition pouch with brass fittings; and light blue overalls with a red stripe and black 'booting'. As for all Carlist mounted units, saddles were usually covered with black or white sheepskins; if valises were issued, they were in jacket colour trimmed with facing-colour braid.

a more 'popular' force than the Army of the North, and until 1838 it presented only a secondary threat to the Liberal government. Cabrera tended to rule the territories under his control as a despot, and showed little interest in collaborating with the Army of the North. In Aragon he was mostly confronted by Liberal militias and paramilitary corps – but only until the Queen Regent's regulars had defeated the Carlists in the north. This partly explains the initial successes of the Army of the Centre, and also its subsequent rapid defeat when it finally faced Gen Espartero's victorious veterans marching south in 1839–40.

In 1837 Cabrera made an attempt to introduce conscription in his territories, but with little practical result. The Army of the Centre remained a mostly volunteer force, although many of its new recruits were deserters from the Liberal militia or unwilling Aragonese former conscripts to the Liberal Army. In June 1834 the Carlist forces in Maestrazgo numbered just 1,500 men and 50 horses; by December 1839, Cabrera commanded 25,000 soldiers with 1,500 horses.

Infantry

As in the north, units were organized on a provincial basis, as single independent battalions with 8 companies (though usually stronger than in the north, with 800–1,000 men). Battalions were grouped into four large divisions, as follows:

Tortosa, 6 line battalions; Aragon, 10 line bns, 1 Tiradores bn, 1 Guides bn; Valencia, 7 line bns; and Turia, 4 line bns, 1 Guides battalion.

Tortosa, located in southern Catalonia close to the border with Aragon, was Cabrera's home city, and the units from this area were extremely loyal. The Tortosa Div was divided into the Mora and Tortosa Bdes, each having 3 battalions. In 1839 the Aragon Div was reorganized in 3 brigades, still with a total of 12 battalions but differently designated (8 line, 3 of Tiradores, and the Guides). Apparently the term 'Tiradores' in this case did not denote any special training or weapons, but was an honorific title for line units that had distinguished themselves in battle. The Turia Div took its name from the river that crosses Valencia, but it was also known as the Murcia Div because many of its soldiers came from that province. Its elite battalion, the 'Guides of Cabrera', was formed in

1839 with former Carlist prisoners exchanged by the Liberals. Two of the division's four line battalions were Castilian.

In addition, the *Miñones de Cabrera* were a 100-strong elite company performing multiple functions under the General Staff, as bodyguards, military policemen, scouts and messengers; their duties were so demanding that the men were discharged after just two years. There were also some company-sized units of naval infantry; these *Compañias de Marina* manned a flotilla of small gunboats operating on the River Ebro, but also included a 20-man mounted escort armed with carbines.

Cavalry

The plains of Aragon were much more suitable for cavalry than the mountainous north, but while horses were more numerous Cabrera's cavalry were still deficient in equipment; perhaps half the troopers had no sabres, and carbines were rare. They were organized in regiments of 3 or 4 squadrons attached to the infantry divisions, as follows:
Tortosa Div, *Lanceros de Tortosa* of 4 sqns, plus elite tiradores company with carbines – the best cavalry unit; Aragon Div, 2 regts each of 3 sqns; Valencia Div, 1 regt of 3 sqns; Turia Div, under-strength *Lanceros del Cid*, including many Castilians.

In addition, in autumn 1839 Gen Balmaseda brought his elite 'Hussars of Ontoria' south when the Army of the North surrendered to Gen Espartero; it now had only 200 men, in a lancer squadron and a carbine-armed tiradores company, but they were well mounted and equipped. Incorporated into the Aragon Div, the unit later expanded to two squadrons.

Attached to the General Staff was a 100-strong carbine-armed company of expert marksmen; these *Ordenanzas del General* were Cabrera's picked bodyguards and dispatch-riders, most being deserters from the Liberal cavalry.

Artillery and Engineers

Until the summer of 1836 artillery was practically non-existent. Cabrera aimed to form at least a battalion, but the lack of guns and of capable men initially limited it to a single company. Other companies were gradually added, up to a maximum of five. After the capture in January 1838 of Morella, which became Cabrera's capital, these formed a battalion based in the city. By this time there were 4 mule-pack mountain batteries (each with 2 guns and 1 howitzer, and each attached to one of the field divisions), plus two wheeled batteries.

The Corps of Engineers began to be organized early in 1838, mainly to construct defences. Its effective development was largely due to an experienced Prussian officer, the Baron von Rahden. Formed into a 1,000-strong battalion, the engineers were usually based in Morella when not taking part in siege operations.

An infantryman of the Carlist Army of the Centre, which captured large stores of these dark blue greatcoats from the Liberals; both the coat collar patches and the trousers are red. Again, he wears a red *boina* over a patterned kerchief knotted around his head. Both the flapped set of cartridge tubes worn on the belly, and the espadrille-type shoes, were seen in all provinces of Spain. His musket may be French, to judge from the brass muzzle-band.

The elite Guides of Aragon were formed with men picked from the ten line battalions of the Army of the Centre's Aragon Division, and may have been Gen Cabrera's best infantry unit. Their uniform is illustrated here as a blue *boina* with yellow roundel and white tassel; a sky-blue shell jacket piped in red, with two-button scalloped cuff flaps; and brown trousers. In place of coats they have large grey mantles.

CARLIST ARMY OF CATALONIA

Despite a long history of Catalonian revolts against the central government in Madrid (the most recent of which had been suppressed only in 1827), the province's Carlists were never able to pose a serious threat to the government. The clamp-down after 1827 had been effective; the local groups were small, fragmented, and desperately short of weapons, and they never produced a leader of the calibre of Zumalacárregui or Cabrera. During 1834 Don Carlos sent three experienced officers into Catalonia to organize and lead them, but all were killed before they could even begin their task.

In 1835 the Catalonian Carlists were finally organized into 4 territorial divisions totalling 23 battalions:

Girona: 3,929 men, of which 83 were horsemen, in 2 infantry brigades, a detached 400-man Guides bn, and a 50-strong lancer squadron.

Lleida: 3,534 men of which 121 horsemen, in 2 inf brigades.

Manresa: 4,212 men of which 55 horsemen, in 2 inf bdes plus a 700-man independent battalion.

Tarragona: 4,209 men including 55 horsemen, in 8 inf battalions.

These were later reduced to 21 battalions, reorganized into 3 divisions each with 5 battalions, plus the remaining 6 in a Reserve Division. In 1838 Don Carlos sent one of his most experienced and capable subordinates, the Count of Spain (a French aristocrat, and ex-governor of Catalonia) to take command. His arrival brought rapid results: objectives were captured, the organization became more regular, and the new commander began a profitable collaboration with the Aragonese forces of Cabrera who controlled the other bank of the Ebro. Through this corridor the Carlists of Maestrazgo were able to send weapons and supplies to the Catalonians. The new commander introduced regular training and severe discipline; he also created a corps of cadets, and a personal bodyguard unit of 60 ex-policemen from the Mossos d'Esquadra. On 20 June 1838 he introduced conscription, and reduced the number of battalions to 14 numbered regular units of a common size. These were assembled in four divisions, now including an elite Vanguard Div intended to serve as a striking force that could operate away from the army's bases (which the other territorial divisions were unable to do).

Thanks to all these positive measures, the insurgent Army of Catalonia could finally be considered as a proper military force. However, the cavalry was still limited to very small units of so-called *'cosacos'* serving only as scouts and couriers, and due to lack of guns the artillery remained insignificant.

CARLIST GUERRILLAS

In addition to the three armies described, the Carlist forces also included large numbers of irregular *guerrilleros* who were initially active across much of Spain. Most of these bands were easily crushed by the government's paramilitary forces early in the war, but in some provinces they remained troublesome for years.

After the Independence War against France ended in 1814, various bands of *guerrilleros* had retained their weapons and continued to operate as common bandits, causing a chronic problem for the monarchy thereafter. In 1833 most of these bands embraced Don Carlos's cause more or less cynically, seeking a patriotic and religious cover for their activities. In the name of the Carlists they conducted against the Liberals the same kind of warfare that they had employed against Napoleon's troops: intercepting supply convoys, cutting communications, harassing columns marching through their territory, attacking small and isolated posts, and raiding for every possible resource. The provinces where these irregulars remained most active after 1834 were Galicia, Old Castile and New Castile, where they could receive some kind of support from the Carlist armies (including weapons and ammunition, with which to fight rival gangs as well as the Liberals).

Some guerrilla leaders tried to emulate the regular Carlist forces, but the only one who nearly achieved this was Jerónimo Merino, who had become famous in Old Castile as *El Cura* ('the parish priest') during the war against Napoleon.[2] During the first weeks of the Carlist insurrections this 64-year-old firebrand formed an 11,000-strong force of 14 infantry battalions, mostly from fellow veterans of the Independence War or ex-Royal Volunteers, with which he even menaced Madrid in October 1833. After being defeated by the Liberals, Merino was obliged to cross the border into Portugal with just 200 men. In March 1834 he returned at the head of a semi-regular squadron of lancers, being nominated by Don Carlos as military commander for the

A Valencian infantryman of the Army of the Centre. Only the first four battalions of that army's Valencia Division were issued proper uniforms (see Plate F2), while the remaining three were mostly dressed in the traditional Valencian costume shown in this drawing. Note the blunderbuss: this sketch probably also suggests the appearance of the poorer sort of local *guerrilleros* in the south-east.

---

2   For more details, see Osprey Elite 108, *Spanish Guerillas in the Peninsular War 1808-14.*

Carlist cavalrymen, all wearing simple shell jackets with coloured collar and cuffs; compare with Plate H. Note the very extensive leather 'booting' that reinforces their overalls, leaving the cloth exposed only on the front and outside of the legs down to the knee. Their equipment is reduced to a minimum: a white canvas bag slung as a haversack, and a black leather crossbelt with an ammunition pouch. In fact Carlist cavalry rarely had firearms, and even sabres were scarce.

province of Old Castile. After two years of intense hit-and-run fighting he went north to recover from ill health, but soon returned to Castile with two lancer squadrons. During 1838 Merino achieved some of his most important successes, but his physical condition finally obliged the old leader to retire.

WEAPONS

In general terms, the Carlists suffered from a serious shortage of weapons and ammunition throughout the war. Unlike the Liberals, they had no possibility of acquiring stocks from abroad, due to the British and French naval blockade. The Pyrenees border was strictly controlled by the French; some supplies got across, but not weapons in any significant numbers. Consequently the Carlists were obliged to use whatever was locally available or could be captured from the Liberal forces.

In the north, the supporters of Don Carlos had a certain advantage in 1833 in that the local Royal Volunteers militia had not already been disarmed by the government, as had been done in Aragon and Catalonia. But these weapons were generally old and in poor condition, and their number was insufficient to equip all the volunteers assembling to form the Army of the North. Many early military actions were launched in order to capture weapons and ammunition, and after any successful engagement the weapons of enemy casualties were systematically collected. Thanks to these measures, and to some successful attacks on enemy arsenals, the Carlist commanders were gradually able to arm at least their infantry to an acceptable level, but ammunition remained a serious problem. Carlist infantrymen usually went into battle with only a few rounds in their pouches; for this reason their tactics tended to limit the use of muskets to skirmishing actions, and emphasized bayonet attacks during pitched battles.

The most common infantry musket was obviously the Brown Bess, together with the French M1777 and various Spanish models captured from the Liberals. Cavalry carbines, pistols and even sabres were very scarce, so almost all Carlist mounted units were formed of lancers: lances were easy and cheap to produce locally, while other weapons mostly had to be acquired on the battlefield. Again, surplus British and French models dating from the Napoleonic wars were the most common, alongside captured Spanish types. Apparently those Carlist troopers who

Naive but useful impression of the Castilian 'Hussars of Ontoria', the crack cavalry unit that rode south to join the Army of the Centre after the collapse of the Army of the North at the end of August 1839. Compare with Plate H1 for appearance, but with uniform colours as follows: the *boina* is shown as dark blue (it had initially been red), with a yellow roundel but no tassel; the unique pelisse is completely made of black fur or fleece, with black loops and toggles; the white dolman has a dark blue collar and pointed cuffs edged with green piping, and all the cording is in mixed red-and-green, including on the rear seams. The overalls are red, apparently without side-stripes or piping. The Ontoria Hussars' lances had black pennons with a white death's-head device.

Artillerymen of the Army of the Centre, transporting a brass mountain gun on two mules. For the uniform colours of the central figure, see Plate F4. The other two gunners are shown wearing the service uniform of Cabrera's artillery: red beret with white tassel; dark blue single-breasted shell jacket, with red piping and epaulettes, and black collar with brass flaming-shell badge; red trousers with black side-stripe (or white summer trousers, right). Note the infantry weapons and belly pouches.

had a sabre were generally equipped with either the British M1796 or Spanish M1822 light cavalry patterns.

The problem was even greater as regards artillery: when the war started, the Army of the North had just a single iron 36-pdr siege gun. By early 1835 Zumalacárregui had 3 field guns, and later he had 3 mountain guns cast from brass objects collected from the population. At the first siege of Bilbao during the early summer of 1835 the Carlists deployed just 5 field guns, 2 howitzers and 1 mortar, and by 1836 these had been augmented to 8 field guns and 9 fixed pieces. In 1837 the Army of the North established its own iron foundry, producing 3 good quality 16cm howitzers, 4x 12cm mountain howitzers (named after the four Carlist provinces), and a single 12-pdr gun. Larger numbers of bronze light howitzers and mortars were also produced in various small factories in the Carlist territories. All the artillery was transported with mules, as horses were too valuable to be used for this purpose.

Until mid-1836 the Army of the Centre had practically no artillery, but around that time it acquired 4 locally produced pieces (2x 4-pdrs and 2x 8-pdrs). In 1838 each of Cabrera's divisions received 2x 4-pdr mountain guns and 2x 7-pdr mortars; he also had perhaps 20 siege and/or fortress guns.

SELECT BIBLIOGRAPHY

Alcalá, Cesar, *Primera Guerra Carlista: El sitio de Bilbao y la Expedicion Real* (Madrid, 2006)

Brett, E.M., *The British Auxiliary Legion in the First Carlist War 1835-1838* (Dublin, 2005)

Bueno, José Maria, *Andalucia y sus Milicia* (Madrid, 1990)

Bueno, José Maria, *Guardias Reales de España desde el reinado de los Reyes Católicos hasta Juan Carlos I* (Madrid, 1989)

Bueno, José Maria, *La Infanteria y la Artilleria de Marina 1537-1931* (Malaga, 1985)

Bueno, José Maria, *Soldados de España: el uniforme militar español desde los Reyes Católicos hasta Juan Carlos I* (Malaga, 1978)

Bueno, José Maria, *Tropas Carlistas, 1833-1840* (Malaga, 1984)

Cairns, Conrad, 'A Savage and Romantic War: Spain 1833-1840. The Course of the First Carlist War', in *Wargames Illustrated* (October 1994)

Cairns, Conrad, '... The Cristino Forces', in *Wargames Illustrated* (November 1994)

Cairns, Conrad, '... The Carlist Army of the North: Infantry '. in *Wargames Illustrated* (February 1995)

Cairns, Conrad, '... The Carlist Army of the North: Cavalry and Artillery', in *Wargames Illustrated* (March 1995)

Cairns, Conrad, '... The Carlist Army of the Centre', in *Wargames Illustrated* (September 1995)

Cairns, Conrad, ' ... The Battle of Oriamendi', in *Wargames Illustrated* (December 1995)

Cairns, Conrad, *The First Carlist War 1833-1840. A Military History and Uniform Guide* (Nottingham, 2009)

Canales Torres, Carlos, *La Primera Guerra Carlista 1833-1840. Uniformes, Armas y Banderas* (Madrid, 2000)

Fiedler, Wacek, 'The Polish lancer regiment in the French Foreign Legion during the First Carlist War', in *The Foreign Correspondent* (October 1998); trans from Jacek Jaworski, 'Pulk Ulanow Polskich Legii Cudzoziemskiej 1836-38 – daieje, barwa i bron' , in *Militaria* nr 6 (Warsaw, 1997)

Gonzalez, R. & Guirao, R., *Guerras Carlistas en Irun y Hondarribia 1833-1876* (Madrid, 2016)

Hernandez, F.X. & Riart, F., *Soldats, Guerrers i Combatents dels Paisos Catalans* (Barcelona, 2014)

Santacara, Carlos, *La primera Guerra Carlista vista por los Britanicos 1833-1840* (Madrid, 2015)

Windrow, Martin, *French Foreign Legion 1831-1871,* MAA 509 (Oxford, 2016)

Fine period drawing of soldiers of the Carlist Army of the North. Note particularly the plate-like appearance of the *boina* when stiffened with an internal hoop, the very full cut of the trousers, and the mantle worn by the cavalryman (left). Typical of the mounted troops of both sides, especially in winter, this was a voluminous cloak with a deep collar, and arm slits under the 'optional' sleeves. The officer (centre) wears a *zammara* over a double-breasted frock coat of conventional cut, worn with both waist and pouch belts. Usually dark blue, frock coats were widely worn by regular Carlist officers, sometimes with added fur collars and/or epaulettes.

PLATE COMMENTARIES

A: EXTERIOR ROYAL GUARD
When the First Carlist War broke out the Royal Guard was dressed in modifications of the 1824 uniforms adopted as part of its reorganization following the *Trienio Liberal*. Ferdinand VII gave his Guard the best weapons and equipment available, and the influence of Napoleon's Imperial Guard is clearly evident in all these uniforms.

A1: Trooper, Regiment of Lancers, 1836
This 1830/35 modification of the 1824 uniform still resembled that of Napoleon's Polish Lancers, but with the crown of the *czapska* now blue rather than red, and with a plain single-breasted *kurtka* instead of the original red plastrons. Note the white Guard braid on the collar and three on the tails, and the *fleur-de-lys* turnback badge. On campaign the *czapska* often had an oilskin cover. By 1835 this campaign dress had became universal for the four mounted Guard regiments apart from the headgear: the Mounted Grenadiers wore a black bearskin (or a hussar-style busby in their *tiradores* company), the Mounted Chasseurs a Russian-style *kiwer* shako, and the Cuirassiers a helmet (see A2).

A2: Trooper, Regiment of Cuirassiers, 1833
The Tiradores company did not wear the cuirass of this parade uniform, and had an additional horse-tail on the back of the helmet. The regiment's use of the cuirass on campaign was formally abolished in 1834. On campaign the white trousers were initially replaced by dark blue, but in 1835 the regiment changed to the same French *garance* red as these other Guard units.

A3: Grenadier, 1st Regiment of Foot Grenadiers, 1833
The four Grenadier regiments formed the Guard's 1st Division; the two Provincial regiments of Grenadiers that formed the 2nd Div alongside the two regiments of Cazadores wore this same uniform with very minor differences (see caption page 7). The 1824 uniform initially had the typical white braids of Guard units across the chest of the coatee; they were abolished in 1834, but retained on the collar, cuffs and back of the tails. Note the unusual configuration of the cuffs, with the red top piping passing across the white *sardinetas*. This uniform had already been simplified in 1830, substituting a white pompon on the left of the bearskin for the original tall white plume; note the gold decorations on the top patch. In 1834 the bearskin was itself replaced with a more practical shako, but apparently remained in use for a bit longer in the two Provincial regiments. Trousers were *garance* red during the winter and white in summer.

A4: Gunner, Squadron of Horse Artillery, 1834
This uniform, in French light cavalry fashion, had distinctive hussar-style cording on the chest and decorative knots on the sleeves and trousers, in yellow for rankers and gold for officers. This tall shako was also worn by the regiment of Mounted Chasseurs until 1835, when it was replaced with the *kiwer*. As the war progressed the uniform was simplified, with the frontal frogging discontinued.

B: LIBERAL INFANTRY
The French-style basic uniform of the Spanish line and light infantry had been adopted in 1828; both branches had the same weapons and equipment, the main difference between them being the uniform colours – dark blue for line infantry and dark green for Cazadores. The universal Napoleonic-style coatee soon proved impractical on campaign, and the infantry started to make wider use of the frock coats and greatcoats already employed in winter.

B1: Sergeant, Naval Infantry, 1834
This uniform was adopted in 1827, when the Naval Infantry and Naval Artillery were amalgamated (note the flaming-shell collar badge). The coatee is of typical infantry cut, but with unit differences. Characteristics of this corps were a red collar, epaulettes (gold for this sergeant), cuff flaps, tail turnbacks and piping; the medium blue shako pompon; an anchor in the design of the brass shako plate, on the coatee tail turnbacks and on the flap of the cartridge pouch; and the yellow *sardineta* braids on the cuffs. Here the red top band of the shako almost hides the red national cockade held by a gold lace loop. These battalions had no elite/ flank companies.

B2: Grenadier, Line Regiment 'Rey', 1836
Due to the harsh weather conditions in the north, the greatcoat, of either dark blue or grey, soon became the standard campaign dress of the regular infantry. It had collar patches in company colours (red for grenadiers, green for the light-company cazadores, and yellow for centre companies), but only flank companies wore epaulettes. They were also distinguished by yellow *sardinetas*, and cuff flaps and piping in company colours. This grenadier is also distinguished by the red tassel and piping on his forage cap. A copy of the French *bonnet de police,* this was often worn on campaign instead of the shako; it was dark blue for both line and light infantry, with company-coloured distinctions. The infantry of the Royal Guard wore this same campaign dress, but with additional white braiding on the forage cap and on the collar and cuffs of the greatcoat.

B3: Sergeant, light company, Cazadores Regiment 'Reina Gobernadora', 1836
The elite 'Queen Regent' Regt was armed throughout with the excellent Baker rifle. As an alternative to the long greatcoat, Spanish infantrymen could wear this practical knee-length frock coat; this too had collar patches and epaulettes in red or green for flank companies – these white epaulettes are the sergeant's distinction. Normally a green pompon and collar patches identified the *tiradores* light company within a *cazadores* light regiment, but in fact all companies of the *Reina Gobernadora* wore green patches. The shako has the usual black oilskin campaign cover.

B4: *Cazador* of a centre company, Regiment 'Cazadores del Rey', 1833
This figure represents the regulation 1828 uniform of the whole infantry. For the line, the dark blue coatee had a white collar, cuff flaps and piping, and uniform-blue collar patches; only flank companies wore coloured collar patches and epaulettes. For the light infantry, as here, the uniform was dark green with yellow distinctions; centre companies wore uniform-green collar patches, and unlike in the line all companies wore epaulettes in company colours, flank companies being distinguished by yellow *sardinetas* on the cuffs. Officially the line infantry had grey trousers and the light infantry dark green, but this might vary on campaign. All units wore white cotton trousers in summer, when the black shoes were usually replaced with the rope-soled shoes known as *alpargatas*.

For Cazador units, as here, the shako had a tall plume in company colour, topped with a pompon that was always green. Line infantry had an inverted arrangement: the plume, always white, rose from a company-colour pompon at its base. Later in the war a shorter plume was introduced, in company colour like the pompon. The top band of the shako was also in company colour, here showing up the red national cockade.

C: LIBERAL CAVALRY

During the war the uniforms of the cavalry saw more changes than those of any other branch. These hardly affected their weapons and equipment, except for the widespread introduction of lances from 1835, both in the line and light regiments, as replacements for the flintlock carbines carried until then.

C1: Trooper, 3rd Line Cavalry Regiment, 1833

The 1824–35 uniform of the line cavalry included a helmet similar to that worn by French cuirassiers. The dark blue coatee had a red collar, pointed cuffs, turnbacks and piping, the collar bearing the regimental number in white metal. Note the brass shoulder scales with wing-like extensions (see also C2). The weapons included the M1815 heavy cavalry sword and M1831 flintlock carbine. Mantles, very popular on campaign especially during winter, were entirely dark blue.

C2: Trooper, 4th Line Cavalry Regiment, 1837

In 1835 the line cavalry adopted this new shorter-tailed coatee in yellow, with blue facings and piping; the brass shoulder scales were retained, but the collar number was discontinued. Since 1834 the tall heavy-cavalry boots and blue breeches had been replaced by these half-boots, worn under grey overalls with black leather reinforcement ('booting'). The helmet was changed from white metal to a black leather model, keeping the black horsehair mane but losing the red plume. A new model of sleeveless cloak was also introduced, in grey. The Carlist 'Merino's Lancers' in Castile uniformed themselves with captured yellow jackets, but substituted red facings for the blue.

C3: Trooper, 4th Light Cavalry Regiment, 1834

This shows the light cavalry uniform officially adopted in 1824 and distributed during the following year. It included a tall, tapering shako with a small red tuft over a white pompon. The light blue single-breasted coatee was faced and piped in red, bearing the regimental number on the collar, and having the usual protective brass shoulder scales. The 'booted' overalls were dark blue, and cloaks were light blue. Weapons were the M1822 light cavalry sabre and M1831 flintlock carbine.

C4: Trooper, 2nd Light Cavalry Regiment, 1838

In 1835 light cavalry units received this new dark green coatee with yellow collar patches, cuff flaps and piping, but retaining brass shoulder scales. They were also issued a new model of shako that was lower and more bell-shaped than the previous pattern; on campaign this was generally covered with black oilskin, except for the green tuft. The new overalls were *garance* red, while the cloaks were of the grey, sleeveless line model.

D: LIBERAL ARMY

This plate illustrates miscellaneous units. The minor components of the Liberal Army were generally dressed similarly to the infantry, albeit with some significant exceptions. The Engineers, for example, were uniformed like the foot artilleryman (D1), but with a white tower badge on the collar instead of the flaming shell, and white *sardinetas* on the cuffs. Additionally, their shako had a white top band, and a white tuft above a half-red, half-white pompon.

D1: Gunner, 1st Foot Artillery Regiment, 1833

The Liberal foot artillery entered the war with this very 'French Napoleonic' uniform, adopted in 1824; all facings and piping are red, and the collar bears a brass flaming-shell badge. During summer, trousers and gaiters were white. From 1828 the horse artillery wore a similar uniform, but with a differently-shaped coatee plastron; their shako was like that of Plate C3, but with a red tuft over a yellow pompon, and red suspension cords with tassels and flounders. (The Carlist artillery wore the same uniform as D1, except for a red *boina* instead of the shako – but see under Plate F4.)

In 1836 both the foot and horse artillery changed to a single-breasted coatee. This retained the red collar, epaulettes

Grenadier of the Liberal Army in everyday service dress, as worn in barracks and for training. The dark blue *bonnet de police*, piped and tasselled red, is worn over a bandana. The cap was so popular that it would soon become distinctive for the Liberal soldier, being nicknamed the *'isabelino'*. The short single-breasted shell jacket is dark blue with brass buttons, and red collar patches, round cuffs, and piping to the three-pointed shoulder straps. The trousers are grey with a red side-stripe, worn with the typical *alpargatas* shoes. The cloth backpack and the leather crossbelt for the pouch are both white, as is the narrow strap or cord over his right shoulder, which may support a slung water flask.

and piping and the collar badge, but the cuffs were now only piped in red for foot artillery, and pointed and solid red for horse artillery. The new trousers were *garance*, being 'booted' overalls for the horse artillery. The horse-gunners kept their shako; it was now adopted by the foot-gunners too, but without the cavalry-type cords.

D2: Trooper, Regiment *'Húsares de la Princesa'*, 1834
This uniform was probably the most elegant and ornate of any in the Liberal Army; sky-blue was apparently the favourite colour of the Queen Regent, who chose it for this unit initially created as a mounted escort for her little daughter. The tall white shako has a yellow top band, a red cockade, a sky-blue falling plume and a brass crowned monogram of mirrored 'I's for Isabella (repeated on the sabretache). The sky-blue dolman is faced in white and frogged with yellow cord; the similarly-corded white pelisse has black fur trim, and the

Liberal Army grenadier in winter campaign dress. The shako has a black oilskin cover buttoned up its left side, but still displays his company's red pompon. The double-breasted blue greatcoat with brass buttons has red collar patches of the scalloped shape called in French *en accolade*, and is embellished with red epaulettes. The red trousers are confined in dark brown gaiters laced at the knee, apparently showing a vertically lined effect, over light brown shoes. The pack and crossbelts are white, and the musket may be either Spanish or French.

sky-blue overalls have black 'booting' and a yellow stripe. The barrel sash is crimson and yellow. On campaign this regiment used a more practical uniform, including a yellow undress coatee similar to that adopted by the line cavalry in 1835 (see Plate C2). By 1838 both uniforms had been completely worn out during harsh field service, and the unit had to adopt surplus British heavy cavalry jackets, of the kind worn by the Union Brigade at Waterloo. The trousers remained the same, while since 1835 the original shako had been replaced by the new light cavalry pattern (see Plate C4).

D3: Line infantryman of a light company, *Milicia Urbana de Madrid*, 1835
The uniforms of the various Urban Militia units were decided by the local authorities in each city or province, but were usually copied from those of the regular infantry and cavalry, with minor differences. The line infantrymen from Barcelona, for example, wore this same uniform but with grey trousers. The top band of the shako, the pompon and tuft, and the epaulettes were in company colours (the latter being worn by centre as well as flank companies); here green and yellow clearly indicate a *cazador*.

D4: Mounted *Carabinero*, 1834
The members of this large and important paramilitary corps had to provide their own horses and equipment, while weapons were issued by the government. This smart uniform, with *kiwer* shako, was used by both foot and mounted Carabineers; note the fringeless contre-epaulettes.

E: FOREIGN CONTINGENTS IN LIBERAL SERVICE
E1: Lancer, British Auxiliary Legion, 1836
The lancers' uniform appears to be almost identical (apart from the yellow cuff flaps) to that of the British Army's lancer regiments since 1831, when the whole line cavalry adopted scarlet coatees. The *czapska* was generally covered with oilskin, or white cloth in summer, with the falling plume removed.

The BAL's line infantry were also dressed in scarlet, with a long-tailed single-breasted coatee which was soon replaced on campaign with a short shell jacket. The collar, round cuffs and coatee turnbacks were yellow (see E2); centre companies had yellow shoulder straps, while grenadier and light companies wore their distinctive shoulder wings. The official headgear was the British M1828 bell-topped shako, with a brass front plate showing the Spanish coat-of-arms; it had a tuft in company colours (red or green for flank companies, white for centre/ fusilier companies). However, the shako was rarely worn on campaign, and was replaced with one of several caps. The first was a Prussian-looking round dark blue forage cap with a crown broader than the headband, a black leather peak (visor), a yellow headband, and a central pompon in company colours; these details were usually hidden by an oilskin or white summer cover. Another was a peakless cap of similar shape; a light blue example is illustrated on page 15. A third type was a smaller, softer, medium-blue peakless cap of the 'pork pie' shape later called a 'Kilmarnock bonnet'. (Though most familiar from the 1850s, it was first described in a British order of 1829.) This was also covered white in summer. Trousers were 'Oxford blue' or charcoal grey during winter and white in hot weather. Uniquely, the Scottish 6th Regt wore the kilt, complete with sporran and hose, and officers wore the full plaid; dress headgear was the Scottish 'mounted' bonnet, with tufts in company colours.

The Rifle Regt was dressed entirely in dark green; the jacket had three rows of white metal buttons and black contre-epaulettes in the style of the British 95th, but with a red collar, pointed cuffs and trouser-stripe echoing the facings of the 60th. Their M1828 shako had a dark green pompon, and all leather equipment was black instead of white. The Artillery had a dark blue peaked forage cap with a red band; a dark blue shell jacket with red collar, shoulder straps and round cuffs; and dark blue trousers with a red side-stripe.

E2: 'Chapelgorri', 1836
The 'Red Caps' initially wore the red *boina* with a grey double-breasted greatcoat and red trousers ; one print also shows canvas gaiters reinforced with brown leather 'greaves'. Once incorporated into Gen Espartero's regular forces, they received this red shako with a light blue-grey top band, pompon and tuft (see page 14). In 1836 the *Chapelgorris* were attached to the British Auxiliary Legion, and replaced their old greatcoats with British red coatees having a yellow collar, round cuffs, shoulder straps, and short turnbacks. Note the use of the typical Carlist 'belly pouch' instead of the regulars' pattern carried on a crossbelt.

E3: Lancer, French Foreign Legion, 1836
This uniform is reproduced from an article by Jacek Jaworski (see Bibliography). Grisot's history of the Legion describes the shako device of yellow crossed lances over a squadron number, the tall heavy-cavalry boots, and also a red-over-yellow lance pennon, while Jaworski suggests this tricolour design. The uniforms of the so-called 'Algerine' Legion's Polish lancers were initially quite elegant; Col Bernelle was accused of wasting his men's back pay on creating a 'toy', but in March 1836 his experience suggested that he could not rely upon his Spanish allies for tactical support. He needed something that at least aspired to be an all-arms force, and this paid dividends at the battle of Inigo (Zubiri) on 1 August 1836: Maj Henryk Krajewski's lancers rolled up the Carlist skirmish line, and the new battery shelled the enemy breastworks before the successful infantry assault.

For the uniform of the Legion's infantry, see MAA 509 *French Foreign Legion 1831–1871*, Plate B3 and page 9. The Legion battery's gunners wore a dark blue *bonnet de police* piped and tasseled in *garance*, and a dark blue *veste* (shell jacket) with red shoulder loops for attaching epaulettes. Their trousers were dark blue with *garance* piping, or white in summer, worn over white spat gaiters. As stores ran out and were not replaced many of the foot troops probably adopted trousers of local cloth, and *alpargatas*; by the winter of 1836/37 the Legion were both ragged and hungry.

E4: Caçador, Portuguese Auxiliary Division, 1835
This soldier is from the crack 1st Bn, 3rd Light Infantry Regiment. The regulations of 25 October 1834 prescribed some significant changes, but the basic uniform colour for the Caçadores remained the traditional brown adopted in 1808, with extended facings including black plastrons, and brass scale epaulettes with black fringes. Regimental distinctions for the 3rd were a scarlet collar piped black, with black cuffs and cuff flaps; the 4th Caçadores had light blue collars and cuff flaps piped black, and black cuffs. For further Portuguese uniform details, see captions to the Knötel plates on pages 17 and 18.

F: CARLIST INFANTRY & ARTILLERY
Carlist infantry uniforms were simple, cheap to produce and practical to wear. A common element was the beret-like felt *boina* cap, as much as 40cm (nearly 16ins) wide, and often stiffened with a hoop of osier. Most had a central roundel of cloth and a tassel in contrasting colours, the tassel usually silver or gold for officers. Different colours distinguished units from various regions. The usual footwear were cloth and rope *alpargatas*, though officers usually had shoes. Personal equipment was reduced to a minimum, for lightness: a white canvas bag *(saco-morral)* often worn like a knapsack, and a leather belly pouch *(canana)* worn on the front of a waistbelt. The latter was usually in the form of up to 20 cartridge-tubes, plus two pockets with additional ammunition, all covered by a deep leather flap. If no scabbard was available, the bayonet was simply thrust through a slit in the belt.

F1: Grenadier, Tortosa Division; Army of the Centre, 1839
The basic uniform garment might be one of three kinds: a double-breasted greatcoat (as here), a double-breasted frock coat (as F4), or a single-breasted shell jacket (as F2). Buttons were usually brass. The greatcoat, worn with the skirts buttoned back, was the most often seen; grey was the commonest colour, but dark blue and brown were also frequently used. Company distinctions were only worn by the battalions of the Tortosa Div; our grenadier is identified as such by a red cap-tassel, collar patches, shoulder rolls and cuff flaps (and note the tips of yellow *sardinetas* showing above the latter). Light companies had green distinctions, and centre companies yellow. During summertime the trousers were generally white, and worn rolled up.

Most Carlist infantry were dressed similarly to this figure. Nearly all the line battalions of the Northern Army (from the provinces of Navarre, Alava, Guipúzcoa, Vizcaya, Cantabria and Castile) wore a blue beret with a yellow roundel and white tassel, a grey frock coat, and red trousers. Only the 5th Guipúzcoa Bn, acting as Royal Guard for Don Carlos, were differentiated by a yellow tassel and additional red collar patches. The 'Guides of Alava' were dressed like the line battalions of their province, but with red berets having yellow roundels and white tassels.

F2: Infantryman, Valencia Division; Army of the Centre, 1839
The first four battalions of this division had dark blue double-breasted greatcoats and white trousers like F1; the remaining three had this dark blue shell jacket with a red collar, and all wore plain dark blue berets. Elements of civilian clothing were popular, especially this kilt-like white *zaraguell*, traditionally worn by the inhabitants of the countryside around Valencia.

F3: Marine, Compañias de Marina; Army of the Centre, 1839
Raised by a relative of Gen Cabrera's, partly from fishermen, these river gunboat units had a smart dark blue coatee with yellow turnbacks and braiding, and dark green trousers with yellow side-stripes. This kind of more elegant uniform was characteristic of elite units. For instance, Don Carlos's *Alabarderos de la Guardia de Honor del Rey* had a blue beret with white tassel; a light blue single-breasted frock coat with red cuff flaps, *sardinetas* (on collar and cuffs) and bands of lace across the chest; and red trousers. When they changed denomination to the *Guardia de Honor de Infanteria* they received a new grey double-breasted frock coat with black collar patches and cuffs (the latter with white *sardinetas*), and grey trousers.

F4: Artilleryman, Army of the Centre, 1839

This illustrates the campaign dress worn by Cabrera's artillerymen: red beret with white tassel; grey double-breasted frock coat with red-piped black collar and cuffs, bearing respectively a flaming-shell badge and two rear buttons; red epaulettes; and red trousers with a black side-stripe. In service dress they wore a dark blue single-breasted jacket with red piping and epaulettes, and the same collar and cuffs as on the frock coat.

When in the field the gunners of the Army of the North dressed somewhat similarly to this figure, but with a black-tasselled blue beret and blue trousers; their coat lacked epaulettes and collar-piping, and had plain grey cuffs. Their parade uniform copied that worn by their Liberal counterparts (see Plate D1), but with a red beret with a black tassel. The Northern Army's elite 1st Artillery Company, attached to the General Staff, had a distinctive dark blue single-breasted

Apart from the ubiquitous grey or dark blue greatcoats, brown examples are also well documented, but were common only in the eastern regions of Spain. This Carlist soldier has a brown coat with a red turn-down collar and pointed cuffs, a dark blue beret, red trousers, and *alpargatas*. A white sash is wound around his waist under the belly-pouch, and he seems to have a slung water canteen made from a dried and hollowed-out gourd.

jacket having red piping and cuff flaps and a black collar with flaming-shell badge, worn with the black-tasselled blue beret and blue trousers.

Carlist engineers of the Northern Army wore a red *boina* without tassel, a light blue double-breasted frock coat having a red collar with a white tower badge, and dark blue trousers. Cabrera's engineers had a red beret with white tassel; a dark blue single-breasted jacket with the white tower badge on the red collar, white epaulettes, and white *sardinetas* on the red cuffs; and white trousers.

G: CARLIST ELITE UNITS & IRREGULARS

G1: Trooper, *'Ordenanzas del General'* Squadron; Army of the Centre, 1839

This mounted escort unit had one of the most elegant uniforms worn in Cabrera's army, and were among the few Carlist troopers to receive carbines. Like other favoured Carlist cavalry units they were dressed in hussar style, with green cording on a red pellise, 'booted' light blue overalls with a red side-stripe, and a green *boina* with yellow roundel and red tassel.

G2: Soldier, *'Miñones de Cabrera'*; Army of the Centre, 1839

The dress of this small elite corps – 'Cabrera's Darlings' – was a copy of that worn by the *Mossos d'Esquadra,* the Catalan paramilitary police, in dark blue with white trim. Note that the belly pouch is worn over a scarlet waist sash passing over the red-brown waistcoat. This was one of the few Carlist uniforms that did not include a *boina*.

Other special units also received distinctive uniforms. In the Army of the North the 'Grenadiers of the Army' Bn had a medium blue beret with yellow roundel and white tassel; a dark blue double-breasted frock coat or a single-breasted shell jacket with white metal buttons and white *sardinetas* on the collar and cuffs; and red trousers. The 'Distinguished Volunteers of Madrid' Bn had a red beret with yellow roundel and white tassel, a plain dark blue double-breasted frock coat, and grey trousers. Don Carlos's Portuguese Bn was the only unit in the Northern Army to wear a green *boina* (without tassel), together with a dark blue coatee with a red collar, cuffs and piping and white Portuguese shoulder rolls, and grey trousers. The *Aduaneros* customs guards had a blue beret with yellow roundel and white tassel, worn with a completely brown suit of a short double-breasted jacket, waistcoat and trousers, a red waist sash, and a profusion of silver buttons.

G3: Soldier, *'Guías de Cabrera'* Battalion; Army of the Centre, 1839

This uniform, based on a medium blue single-breasted frock coat with a red collar and white *sardinetas* above the cuff, was worn by the crack Guide unit of the Turia Division. The line battalions of that division wore a blue *boina* with yellow roundel and no tassel; a dark blue shell jacket with red collar, cuffs, piping, and edging to the pockets; and white trousers. In the Army's Aragon Div the Guides Bn were distinguished by a blue beret with yellow roundel and white tassel; a sky-blue shell jacket with red cuff flaps and piping; and brown trousers. The Aragon Div's line battalions wore the same beret but with a red tassel; a dark brown shell jacket piped in red; and white trousers.

G4: *Guerrillero,* New Castile, 1837

The irregular insurgents operating in Castile dressed in the civilian clothing of the region, generally sporting many silver buttons and various other decorative elements. Note the distinctive hat worn over a colourful kerchief, the sturdy buckled riding gaiters, and the traditional Spanish spurs with large revolving rowels. Multiple weapons were typically carried, including sabres, daggers, flintlock pistols and short blunderbusses. (Indeed, *guerrilleros* operating in Liberal-held provinces were often more heavily armed than Carlist regular soldiers.)

H: CARLIST CAVALRY

Almost all Carlist mounted units were equipped with locally-made lances; pennons were usually red over yellow, though red over white was also seen, and 'Merino's Lancers' uniquely had red over black. Most units wore a single-breasted short coatee or shell jacket. Collar, pointed cuffs and the turnbacks of coatee tails were in a contrasting colour, but sometimes only collar patches and cuff piping were evident. Overalls could be of various colours, usually 'booted' with black leather. Spurs were of the traditional Spanish type, bigger than those used by the Liberal cavalry. Winter cloaks were generally grey or blue, sometimes with coloured collars.

H1: Trooper, 'Húsares de Arlában' Squadron; Army of the North, 1836

Initially the single cavalry squadron from Alava wore a light blue coatee with red collar patches, turnbacks and piping, but it later received this hussar uniform while retaining the original *boina:* white dolman and pelisse faced with light blue, corded in mixed red and light blue, and red overalls with a light blue stripe.

H2: Lancer, Valencian cavalry; Army of the Centre, 1839

This is typical of the appearance of Carlist lancers, though the regiment from Valencia lacked some equipment and dress, including military overalls and sometimes even boots. The same was true of the *Lanceros del Cid* in the Turia Div, who probably fought in civilian clothing.

H3: Lancer, Navarrese cavalry; Army of the North, 1835

These were the core of the Northern Army's cavalry, despite their chronic shortage of good horses and carbines. The other squadrons of the Army of the North were dressed quite similarly, but with different colours. The Aragonese cavalry were dressed like this but with yellow-piped overalls. The cavalry from Vizcaya had a red beret, brown coatee with red piping, and red trousers. 'Merino's Lancers' differed in having a yellow coatee with red collar patches and pointed cuffs, and grey trousers. The squadron from Guipúzcoa wore a red hussar-style pelisse instead of the coatee, with black fur, cording and elbow patches; this was worn with a white beret, and grey trousers. The squadrons from Castile were dressed like the Navarrese, but their coatees might also be brown instead of green. The *Escolta para el Estandarte de la Generalísima* had the same uniform as the 'Honour Guard of Cavalry' (see caption page 34), except for white epaulettes, collar patches and pouch belt. The 'Squadron of Commanders and Officers' wore the same *boina*; a dark blue long-tailed coatee with red piping, turnbacks, collar and cuffs (both having the additional silver braids typical of Spanish guard units), silver contre-epaulettes and aiguilettes, light blue trousers with a silver side-stripe, and a red and silver pouch belt.

H4: Tirador, 'Lanceros de Tortosa' Regiment; Army of the Centre, 1839

Only the carbine-armed *tiradores* company of this elite regiment wore this yellow hussar-style uniform with green

facings and cording, and a sky-blue beret and overalls. The other troopers were dressed and equipped as normal lancers, with a white beret with yellow roundel and mixed yellow-red tassel; a sky-blue coatee with red collar patches, turnbacks and piping, and brass shoulder scales; and grey overalls with a yellow stripe.

This Aragonese cavalryman wears a uniform in the same colours as Plate H3, but with a turn-down collar, and yellow piping to the red overalls.

INDEX